John Reade

The prophecy of Merlin

and other Poems

John Reade

The prophecy of Merlin
and other Poems

ISBN/EAN: 9783743303652

Manufactured in Europe, USA, Canada, Australia, Japa

Cover: Foto ©Thomas Meinert / pixelio.de

Manufactured and distributed by brebook publishing software
(www.brebook.com)

John Reade

The prophecy of Merlin

THE

PROPHECY OF MERLIN

AND

OTHER POEMS.

BY

JOHN READE.

MONTREAL:
PUBLISHED BY DAWSON BROTHERS.

———

1870.

MONTREAL : PRINTED BY THE MONTREAL PRINTING AND PUBLISHING CO.

" O living friends that love me !

O dear ones gone above me !

Careless of other fame,

I leave to you my name.

*   *   *   *

Sweeter than any sung

My songs that found no tongue ;

Nobler than any fact

My wish that failed of act."

J. G. Whittier.

CONTENTS.

ESSAYS IN TRANSLATION.

Hector and Andromache,—   PAGE

    The Parting · · · · · · · 181

    The Lament of Andromache · · · · 189

The Beacon Light · · · · · · · 194

Priam and Helen · · · · · · · · 198

Song of the Trojan Captive · · · · · · 205

Bellerophon · · · · · · · · · 208

Horace, Ode xi. Book I. · · · · · · 211

Orpheus and Eurydice · · · · · · · 212

Adrian's Address to his Soul · · · · · 217

Pyramus and Thisbe · · · · · · · 219

The Withered Leaf · · · · · · · 225

André Chenier's Death-song · · · · · · 226

The Lake · · · · · · · · · 229

The Wandering Jew· · · · · · · · 233

POEMS.

THE PROPHECY OF MERLIN.

Sir Bedivere, in silence, watched the barge
That bore away King Arthur to the vale
Of Avalon, till it was seen no more.
Then, on the beach, alone amid the dead,
He lifted up his voice and sorely wept.
" Alas !" he cried, " gone are the pleasant days
At Camelot, and the sweet fellowship
Of noble knights and true, and beauteous dames
Who have no peers in all the living world,
Is quite dissolved for ever, and the King
Has gone and left none like him among men.
O happy, thrice and fourfold, ye who rest,
Both friends and foemen, in one peaceful bed,
While I am sick at soul and cannot die !
Oh ! that the battle might be fought again !
Then would I surely seek the way to death,

And bleed and sleep like you, and be at peace.

But now, ah ! whither, whither can I go,

Since he is gone who was my light of life,

And whom to see was bliss ?   What can I do

Without the voice that gave my arm its strength ?

Or wherefore bear a sword, since now no more

Excalibur points forth to noble deeds ? "

And then he drew his blade, and threw it far

Into the Lake, and, as he saw it sink,

" Would God," said he, " that so I followed him."

But with the strain his wounds began to bleed,

And he grew weak, and sank upon the ground,

And swooned.

                 And when he woke, he was aware

Of Merlin, who stood watching by his side.

Then cried Sir Bedivere : " O good and wise,

I bid thee welcome, for, in all the world,

There is none other I would fainer see.

Yet am I sad to see thee, for the King

Is gone, and none is left of all his Knights

Save me, and I am weary of my life."

But Merlin, ere he answered, staunched his wound,
And gave him wine out of a golden flask,
And, by the healing art which he possessed,
Restored him sound and whole. And then he spake :
" There is no need to tell me, for I know
All thou would'st say, and knew ere thou wast born
That all these things should be. But weep no more,
Sir Bedivere. The past no man can change,
Nor make what has been other than it is.
As in the forests of Broceliande,
The leaves fall year by year, and give the oaks
All bare to wintry blasts, so, swept apace
Before the breath of Time, the race of men
Passes away, and may be seen no more.
And yet the breeze of Spring is no less sweet,
Which plays around the tender budding leaves,
And calls to life their beauty, that it is
As well a requiem as baby-song.
So weep not for the days that are no more,
But pray, as the King bade thee, for his soul,
That to his far-off home no sigh may come
From this, his orphan and unhappy realm,
To mar the melody of Avalon,"

Then said Sir Bedivere : " O good and wise,
Will he return again to Camelot,
After his wound is healed, and Guinevere
Has healed that other wound that vexed his soul,
By purging her own soul of all offence?
And will he not assemble round his board
The best and bravest knights of Christendom,
And all the fairest ladies of the land,
And reign as erst he reigned in Camelot ? "

Then Merlin : " Hid from eyes of common men
Is that which is to be in after days ;
And only those can see it in whose souls
A heavenly brightness has dissolved the mist
That darkens mortal sight. And even these
Can see but dimly, as a far-off hill
Appears at even when the stars surprise
The lingering kisses of the parting sun.
But I, thou knowest well, Sir Bedivere,
Am not of mortal race, nor was I born
Of human mother nor of human sire.
Mine is the blazonry of prophet souls

Whose lineage finds in God its kingly head.

To me what was and that which is to come

Are ever present, and I grow not old

With time, but have the gift of endless youth.

As one who stands beside a placid stream,

Watching the white sails passing slowly down,

And knows a fatal whirlpool waits them all,

And yet, the while, is powerless to save,—

So watch I all the ages passing by

Adown the stream of time into the gulf

From which is no return. Alas! alas!

How oft have I, who ever love the good,

The pure, the brave and wise, wept bitter tears,

As they have passed me, joyous in their course,

And we have held sweet converse, as I thought

How soon their faces would be seen no more!

Sad, sad, Sir Bedivere, the prophet's gift,

Who sees the evil which he cannot heal!"

And then a gloom o'ershadowed Merlin's face,

That caused Sir Bedivere to pity him;

And they both wept, as one, amid the dead,

Thinking of all the sorrows of the world.

But Merlin, when his face grew calm again,
Began : " Come, hearken now, Sir Bedivere,
And I will give an answer to thy quest :
King Arthur sleeps in Avalon, and many a change
Must over-pass this land before he wake.
The great White Dragon of the stormy North,
Rearing his crest above the foaming waves,
Shall shake the ground, and level all the hills,—
And war shall follow war,—and blood shall flow
In every vale,—and smoke of burning towns
Shall reach the sky,—and men shall cry for aid
Unto the sea, to hide them from the foe—
And still shall Arthur sleep in Avalon.

And when the Dragon, sated with the blood
Of Christian men and women, yields at length
To a mild victor, Tigers of the Sea
Shall come, from craggy homes, to rend and tear,
And brave men's hearts shall quail before their eyes—
Yet still shall Arthur sleep in Avalon.

The Tigers' wrath appeased, another foe
Shall wave a foreign banner o'er the land,

And trample down beneath his horses' hoofs
Briton, and Dane, and Saxon, till the ground
Is rank with blood, as when upon the slopes
Of Badon Arthur charged the heathen host—
Yet still the King shall sleep in Avalon.

But as the ages pass, these foes shall join
In friendship, and a nation shall arise,
Like a strong oak amid the forest trees,
Which, growing slowly, ceases not to grow,
But fastens firmly, as it aims aloft,
And spreads its branches far on every side,
A shelter to the stranger of all lands—
While Arthur still sleeps on in Avalon.

And many Kings shall rule and win renown
For this now saddened and distracted realm ;
And Britain shall be great by land and sea,
And stretch her conquering arms around the world,
And gather treasures from all climes, and teach
Her tongues to distant nations, and her name
Shall be a word of praise to all the earth—
While Arthur still sleeps on in Avalon.

A*

But though he sleep, he still shall wear the crown
As rightful lord of Britain, for on him,—
The image of a noble Christian King,
The image of a ruler sent of God,—
The people still shall look in whoso reigns.
And if there be a King of soul impure—
Or if there be a King of hand unjust—
Or if there be a King who weighs himself
Against the nation's weal (such Kings there are
And ever shall be until Arthur wake),—
It is the *real* King the people serve,
The Blameless Prince that never can do wrong,
And not the false usurper of his name."

Then, wondering much, broke in Sir Bedivere:
" O Merlin, thou art far too wise for me,
Though well I love thy speech. But, in good sooth,
And plainly, as we speak of common things,
Answer me : Will the King come back again
In his own fleshly guise, the very same
As when he feasted erst in Camelot
With all the Table Round ? And will he wear
Th crown, and gird him with Excalibur,

And conquer heathen foes, and rid the land
Of all that speaketh lies or doeth wrong?—
Or, must he sleep for ever, and his face
Be hid away from those that love him well?
For, if I thought that it were so to be,
I never could have comfort in my life."

Then answered Merlin : " Let me tell my tale
In my own way, and hearken till the close.
All these things happen not as we desire,
But as the ages need.   Such men as he
Come not without great travail and sore pain ;
They are the ripe fruit of the centuries,
Who nourish noble thoughts and noble deeds,
Give health and vigour to the sickly times,
And stir the gross blood of the sleepy world ;
And when they pass away, their names, endued
With life, still head the van of truth and right
So shall the name and spirit of the King,
Who ruled in Camelot the Table Round,
Guide Britain into ever-growing fame ;
And all her Kings that reign shall reign in him,
The golden type of kingly chivalry.

And those three Queens thou sawest, three fair Queens,

So sweet and womanly, who, in the barge,

Bore, tenderly, away the wounded King,

Shall reign in Britain in the after-time,—

As, in the old time, Carismandua

And brave Bonduca whom the Romans feared

Held a firm sceptre in a gentle hand.

Of best and purest Queenhood, they, the type,

As Arthur is the type of Blameless Kings.

And as by three sweet names of holy kin

They shall be known, so shall they also shew

A triple sisterhood beneath one crown—

Britain, and Albyn, and green Innisfail.

Now, when the last of three Queens has slept

For many years, there shall arise a Fourth—

Fair, good and wise, and loved by all the land

Of Britain, and by many lands on every sea.

And in her days the world shall have much changed

From that which now we live in. Mysteries,

Save unto me in vision, now unknown,

Shall then be clear as day. The earth and air

Shall yield strange secrets for the use of men,—

The planets, in their courses, shall draw near,
And men shall see their marvels, as the flowers
That grace the meads of Summer,—time and space
Shall know new laws, and history shall walk
Abreast with fact o'er all the peopled world :—
For words shall flash like light from shore to shore,
And light itself shall chronicle men's deeds.
Great ships shall plough the ocean without sail,
And steedless chariots shoot with arrowy speed
O'er hill and dale and river, and beneath
The solid floor we tread,—the silent rocks
Shall tell the story of the infant world,—
The falling leaf shall shew the cause of things
Sages have sought in vain—and the whole vast
Of sight and sound shall be to men a school
Where they may learn strange lessons ; and great truths
That long have slept in the deep heart of God
Shall waken and come forth and dwell with men,
As in the elder days the tented lord
Of countless herds was taught by angel-guests.
And this fair land of Britain then shall be
Engrailed with stately cities,—and by streams
Where now the greedy wolf roams shall be heard

The multitudinous voice of Industry,—
And Labour, incense-crowned, shall hold her court
Where now the sun scarce touches with his beams
The scattered seeds of future argosies,
That to the furthest limit of the world
Shall bear the glory of the British name.
And where a Grecian victor never trod,
And where a Roman banner never waved,
East, West, and North, and South, and to those Isles,
Happy and rich, of which the poets dreamed
But never saw, set far in Western seas,
Beyond the pillars of the heathen god—
Shall Arthur's realm extend, and dusky Kings
Shall yield obeisance to his conquering fame.

And She, the fourth fair tenant of the throne,
Heir to the ripe fruit of long centuries,
Shall reign o'er such an empire, and her name,
Clasping the trophies of all ages, won
By knightly deeds in every land and sea,
Shall be VICTORIA.
            Then shall come a Prince
From o'er the sea, of goodly mien and fair,

And, winning her, win all that she has won—
Wedded to her, be good as she is pure—
Reigning with her, be wise as she is great—
And, loving her, be loved by all the world."

Then spake Sir Bedivere, all eagerly :
" He, Merlin, is he not our Blameless King,
Returned from his long sleep in Avalon,
To crown the glories of the later world ? "

Then Merlin : " Wait a while, Sir Bedivere,
And I will tell thee all.
     In deeds of war,—
The rage of battle, and the clangorous charge
Of mailéd knights, and flash of hostile swords,
And flying spears, and din of meeting shields,
And all the use of man-ennobling might
For Christ and for His Cross, to wrest the land
From heathen foes—did Arthur win his fame.
For this, by marvels, was he born and bred ;
For this, by marvels, was he chosen King ;
For this he sent his heralds to all parts
Of the divided realm, to summon forth

All bravest, truest knights of Christendom
From rude and selfish war to Camelot,
That they might be one heart around himself
To send new life-blood through the sickly land,
And purge it of the plague of heathennesse.
And had not the foul falsehood of his house
Broken athwart the true aim of his life,
And set the Table Round against itself,
Ere now the heathen Dragon had been crushed,
Never again to raise its hideous head
O'er the fair land that Christ's apostle blessed.

This was the purpose that his soul had formed—
Alas ! how unaccomplished !—and he hoped
That gentle peace would be the meed of war,—
That 'neath the laurel far and wide would bloom
The flowers of wisdom, charity and truth,—
That holy men and sages, ladies fair
And famous knights, and those that from earth's lap
Gather God's bounties, and the men whose hands
Have skilful touch, and those who tell or sing
Of Nature and her marvels, or who fill
The scroll with records of the misty past,

And others of all arts and all degrees,

Should work, each in the place that he had found,

With one pure impulse in the heart of all,—

That Britain should be called of all the world

A blameless people round a Blameless King.

This purpose Albert, in the after-time,

(So shall the Prince be named of whom I spake,)

Shall take from the dim shrine where it has lain,

Scarce touched by dreamy reverence, many an age,

And hold it in the daylight of his life.

But not alone. She whom his heart has won,

With loving aid, shall ever at his side

(Till death them part) sustain him in his thought.

And these two, nobly mated, each to each

The sweet and ripe completion, shall be named

With loyal love and tenderest respect

By knight and lady, poet, sage and priest,

In mart and camp, in palace and in cot,

By babbling gray-beard and by lisping child,

Wherever Britain's banner is unfurled.

So shall the land grow strong with bonds of peace,

Till men believe that wars have ceased to drench

The earth with bloody rain ;—and Art shall smile
On myriad shapes of beauty and of use,—
And Wisdom shall have freer scope, and push
The boulders of old folly from her field,—
And men shall walk with larger minds across
The limits of the superstitious past,
And cull the gold out of the dross of things,
Flinging the dross aside,—and then shall be
New hopes of better changes yet to be,
When harmony shall reign through all the world,
And interchange of good for common weal
Be only law.

        A palace shall arise
Beneath the guidance of the Blameless Prince,
The crystal image of his ample mind,
The home of what is best in every clime ;
And thither, from all lands beneath the sun,
Shall crowd the patient workers in all arts,
Bringing the treasures of their skill. The hands
Of many nations with a brother's clasp
Shall join together ; and the Babel tongues
Of Eastern, Western, Northern, Southern lands
Shall strive no more in discord, but, as one,

Shall make harmonious music, as of yore
The sound of four great rivers rose and fell
Through fragrant splendours in the Eden-world.

And men shall say : 'Now is the reign of peace,
Foretold by sacred sages, come at last.
And cries of war shall never more be heard
Through the fair world, but men shall take their swords
And beat them into ploughshares, and their spears
And lances they shall turn to pruning-hooks,—
Nation with nation shall contend no more,
Save as to who may reach the goal of best
Before the other, for the common good,—
And men shall only vie in virtue, skill
And beauty, fruits of hand and head and heart,—
And strength shall be in knowlege and its use,—
And right, not might, shall guide men in their acts,—
And small and great shall have one common law,—
And he, alone, shall be considered just
Who, in a doubtful matter, puts himself
In his friend's place. So all men shall be friends :
For each shall see in other but himself,
And love him as himself. This is Christ's rule,

Which the base world so long has set at nought,
But now restored by our All-blameless Prince,
And preached by gentle act to all the world.'

So shall men say, rejoicing ; but, alas !
While yet the words rise from their gladdened hearts,
The olive garland shall begin to fade
On the sweet brows of peace ; and Avarice,
Like a gaunt wolf, ever unsatisfied
As long as one lamb bleats within the fold,
Shall raise the harsh cry that awakens war.

In those far lands beyond the Southern Sea,
Traversed by knights who seek the Holy Grail,
The mountains belch forth fire, and flood the slopes
And valleys with the sulphurous tide of hell,
Till man and all his works are whelmed beneath.
Then, wearied with his rage, the demon sleeps,
And o'er the frozen graves of the long dead
The hopeful vine grows and the flowers bloom,
And children's voices and the song of birds
Bid hush the awful memory of the past.

But on some doomful night an ominous roar
Startles the dreaming villager, who, looking
Forth through his shivering casement, sees the sky
Alive with fearful forms. The spirits of fire,
Unchained from their long bondage, with fierce joy
Dance onward, bearing death, while smoky palls
Waver around them. With their ghostly hands
From wrathful vials they pour blazing streams
That lick the earth, from which is no escape
But death—and death comes soon. So after peace,
Which men had thought eternal, shall come war,
And chase, with rumbling horror, the sweet dreams
Of gentle harmony throughout the world.

Then shall the spirit of the Table Round
Enter men's hearts and make their right arms strong
For deeds of war,—deeds that shall make the eyes
Of those who come thereafter flash with pride.

By many a far-off height and river-side
Shall fall such men as fought at Badon-hill
Warring with heathen foes ; and lonely hearths
Shall sorrow for the dead who come no more.

And, one war over, others shall succeed,
And others ; and the blaze of burning towns
Shall blot the moon out of the midnight sky.

And some will say : 'Now is the end at hand
Of all things, and the whole fair world is doomed
To sink in ashy nothingness. The wrath
Of God is kindled for the sins of men.'

But when the fiery wave of war has washed
The world, as gold from which the dross is burned,
The nations shall rise purer, and men's hearts
Shall fear the touch of wrong ; the slave ashamed
And angry once to see the pitiless sun
Smile on his chains, shall leap and sing for joy.
Free thought shall take the ancient shield of Truth
And make it bright, showing the Artist's work,
Long hid by stains and rust from longing eyes ;
And hoary ills shall die, and o'er their graves
Shall bloom fair flowers, and trees of goodly fruit
To gladden and make strong the heart of man."

Then said Sir Bedivere : "O, good and wise,

My heart is full of wonder, and I doubt
Whether or not I listen in a dream
Wrought by thy wizard spells around my soul.
But tell me further of the Blameless Prince,
The image of King Arthur,—or himself,
Albeit thou sayst it not, come back again
From his long sleep in Avalon. Shall he die,
Or shall he live and teach men how to live
Until the coming of our Master, Christ?"

Then Merlin, with a cloud upon his face,
As thinking of the sorrow that must be,
Yet with a silver smile about the cloud,
Answered Sir Bedivere: " O, loving well
And loyal to the last, the Blameless Prince,
The God-sent promise of a better time
When all men shall be like him, good and wise,
Shall, when his work is finished, pass away ;
And the dark shade of sorrow's wings shall blot
The sky, and all the widowed land shall mourn ;
And chiefly she, his other self, the Queen,
Shall weep long years in lonely palace-halls,
Missing the music of a silent voice.

But, though his voice be silent, in men's hearts
Shall sink the fruitful memory of his life,
And take deep root, and grow to glorious deeds.
And she will write the story of his life
Who loved him, and though tears may blot the page,
Even as they fall, the rainbow hues of hope
Shall bless them with Christ's promise of the time
When they that sow in tears shall reap in joy."

Then, sad and sore amazed, Sir Bedivere :
" O, Merlin, Merlin, truly didst thou say
That hid from eyes of common men like me
Is that which is to be in after days ;
For even now I scarce can comprehend
What thou hast spoken with prophetic lips.
These things are very far beyond my reach.
This only do I know, that I am now
An orphan knight, reft of the royal sire
That made me knight, giving my soul new birth
And heirdom to the Christian fellowship
Of the Round Table. Gladly would I give
All glory ever won by knightly deed,
All honour in the ranks of my compeers,

All gentle blandishments of ladies fair,
All that I am, or have, or prize the most,
And sink into the meanness of the churl
That feeds the Saxon's swine, for but one glimpse
Of my loved lord, King Arthur. But I know
That he will never more to Camelot
Bring back the glory of his vanished face,
Nor call me his 'true knight, Sir Bedivere.'
So I will pray, even as thou badst me pray,
And as King Arthur bade me, for his soul,
That to his far-off home no sigh may come,
From this his orphan and unhappy realm,
To mar the melody of Avalon.
And though he may not hither come to me,
May I not hope that I may go to him,
And see him face to face, in that fair land,
Whose beauty mortal eye has never seen,
Whose music mortal ear has never heard,
Whose glory mortal heart has not conceived.

But, Merlin, I would ask thee one thing more,
If thou have patience with my blunter sense
(For I am but a knight, and thou, a sage,

B

And knowest all things)—prithee, tell me, Merlin,
If, in the far-off after-time, shall come
A Prince who shall be known by Arthur's name,
And bear it blamelessly as he did his."

Then, Merlin, with a wise smile on his face,
Such as a mother wears who gently tries
To answer the hard question of her child,
Answered Sir Bedivere : " Thou askest well,
And fain am I to answer. That good Prince
Of whom I spake—Albert, the Blameless Prince—
Shall be the head of many dynasties.
His blood, in after years, shall wear the crown
Of many kingdoms. She who loved him well
Shall reign for many years when he is gone,
And round her widowed diadem shall gleam
The richer halo of a nation's love,
For her own sake and for the sainted dead.
And she will shed the brightness of her soul
On Britain's future Kings, and they shall learn,
Not only from her lips, but from her life,
That who rules well must make Christ's law his rule.
And of the Good Queen and the Blameless Prince

One son shall be named Arthur. Like the King
For whom thy heart is sad, Sir Bedivere,
He shall be true, and brave, and generous
In speech and act to all of all degrees,
And win the unsought guerdon of men's love.

In a far land beneath the setting sun,
Now and long hence undreamed of (save by me
Who, in my soul's eye, see the great round world
Whirled by the lightning touches of the sun
Through time and space),—a land of stately woods,
Of swift broad rivers, and of ocean lakes,—
The name of Arthur,—him that is to be,—
(Son of the Good Queen and the Blameless Prince),
Shall shed new glories upon him we loved."

Then, by the memories of his lord, the King,
Sir Bedivere was quickened into tears,
But, like a boy ashamed to shew wet eyes
Before a boy, he passed his mailéd hand
Athwart his face, and frightened back his grief.
And seeing Merlin made no sign to speak
More of the Arthur of the after-time,

He took the word : "Thanks, Merlin, thou art kind
Beyond the limit of my gratitude,
I fear me.   Sorrow is a selfish thing,
And much exacts from friendship.   Still, I thank thee
That thou hast not gainsayed my utmost quest.
And, now, I pray God bless him when he comes,
That other Arthur.   May he keep his name
As pure as his who ruled in Camelot ;
May he, in every wise, be like to him,
Save in the pain that comes of love deceived
And trampled faith ; and may his far-off land
Be great by noble deeds of noble men.".

Then came a sound of music from the Lake,
Like the soft sighing of the summer winds
Among the pine-trees, and Sir Bedivere
Turned toward the sound.   But as he turned again
To ask of Merlin what the music meant,
Merlin was gone, and he was all alone—
Alone upon the beach amid the dead !

DEVENISH.

I.

'Twas years since I had heard the name,
When, seen in print, before my eyes
The old Round Tower seemed to rise,
With silent scorn of noisy fame.

II.

Our little boat, like water-bird,
Touches the still Lake, breast to breast ;
No sound disturbs the solemn rest
Save kiss of oar and whisper'd word.

III.

All Nature wears a placid smile
Of gold and blue and tender green ;
And in the setting of the scene
Lies, like a gem, the Holy Isle.

B*

IV.

Hushed is the music of the oar ;
    A little hand is placed in mine ;
    My blood runs wildly, as with wine—
We stand together on the shore.

V.

O boyish days ! O boyish heart !
    In vain I wish you back again !
    O boyish fancy's first sweet pain,
How glorious, after all, thou art !

VI.

The old Round Tower, the ruined walls,
    Where mould'ring bones once knelt in prayer,
    The Latin legend, winding stair,—
These any " tourist's book " recalls.

VII.

But, oh ! the love, the wild delight,
    The sweet romance of long ago,
    All these have vanished, as the glow
Of eventide fades out at night.

KINGS OF MEN.

As hills seem Alps, when veiled in misty shroud,
   Some men seem kings, through mists of ignorance ;
Must we have darkness, then, and cloud on cloud,
   To give our hills and pigmy kings a chance ?
Must we conspire to curse the humbling light,
   Lest some one, at whose feet our fathers bowed,
Should suddenly appear, full length, in sight,
   Scaring to laughter the adoring crowd ?
Oh, no ! God send us light !—Who loses then ?
   The king of slaves and not the king of men.
True kings are kings for ever, crowned of God,
   The King of Kings,—we need not fear for them.
'Tis only the usurper's diadem
   That shakes at touch of light, revealing fraud.

VASHTI.

"After these things, when the wrath of King Ahasuerus was appeased, he remembered Vashti."—*Book of Esther* ii. 1.

I.

Is this all the love that he bore me, my husband,
    to publish my face
To the nobles of Media and Persia, whose hearts
    are besotted and base?
Did he think me a slave, me, Vashti, the Beautiful,*
    me, Queen of Queens,
To summon me thus for a show to the midst of
    his bacchanal scenes?

II.

I stand like an image of brass, I, Vashti, in sight
    of such men!
No, sooner, a thousand times sooner, the mouth of
    the lioness' den,

---

* Vashti means "*Beautiful Woman*;" Esther means "*A Star.*"

When she's fiercest with hunger and love for the
    hungry young lions that tear
Her breasts with sharp, innocent teeth, I would
    enter, aye, sooner than there !

III.

Did he love me, or is he, too, though the King,
    but a brute like the rest ?
I have seen him in wine, and I fancied 'twas then
    that he loved me the best ;
Though I think I would rather have one sweet,
    passionate word from the heart
Than a year of caresses that may with the wine
    that creates them depart.

IV.

But ever before, in his wine, towards me he shewed
    honour and grace,—
He was King, I was Queen, and those nobles he
    made them remember their place ;

But now all is changed : I am vile, they are
    honoured, they push me aside,—
A butt for Memucan, and Shethar, and Meres,
    gone mad in their pride !

    *   *   *   *   *

V.

Shall I faint ? shall I pine ? shall I sicken and die
    for the loss of his love ?
Not I ; I am queen of myself, though the stars
    fall from heaven above—
The stars ! ha ! the torment is there, for my light
    is put out by a *Star*,
That has dazzled the eyes of the King and his
    Court and his Captains of War.

    *   *   *   *   *

VI.

He was lonely, they say, and he looked, as he sat
    like a ghost at his wine,
On the couch by his side, where, of yore, his
    Beautiful used to recline.

But the King is a slave to his pride, to his oath,
    and the laws of the Medes,
And he cannot call Vashti again, though his poor
    heart is wounded and bleeds.

VII.

So they ransacked the land for a wife, while the
    King thought of me all the while—
I can see him, this moment, with eyes that are lost
    for the loss of a smile,
Gazing dreamily on as each maiden is temptingly
    passed in review,
While the love in his heart is awake with the
    thought of a face that he knew !

    *   *   *   *   *

VIII.

Then *she* came, when his heart was grown weary
    with loving the dream of the past !
She is fair—I could curse her for that, if I thought
    that this passion would last !

But, e'en if it last, all the love is for me, and,
    through good and through ill,
The King shall remember his Vashti, shall think
    of his Beautiful still.

    *   *   *   *   *

IX.

Oh ! the day is a weary burden, the night is a
    restless strife,—
I am sick to the very heart of my soul of this
    life—this death in life !
Oh ! that the glorious, changeless sun would draw
    me up in his might,
And quench my dreariness in the flood of his
    everlasting light !

    *   *   *   *   *

X.

What is it ? Oft, as I lie awake and my pillow is
    wet with tears,
There comes—it came to me just now—a flash,
    then disappears :

A flash of thought that makes this life a re-enacted
  scene,
That makes me dream what was, shall be, and what
  is now, has been.

XI.

And I, when age on age has rolled, shall sit on
  the royal throne,
And the King shall love his Vashti, his Beautiful,
  his own ;
And for the joy of what has been and what again
  shall be,
I'll try to bear this awful weight of lonely misery !

*   *   *   *   *

XII.

The star ! the star ! oh ! blazing light that burns
  into my soul !
The star ! the star ! oh ! flickering light of life
  beyond control !
O King ! remember Vashti, thy Beautiful, thy own,
Who loved thee and shall love thee still, when
  Esther's light has flown !

c

SHAKSPERE.

April 23rd, 1864.

I.

To-day, three hundred years ago,
  A common, English April morn,
  In Stratford town a child was born,
Stratford, where Avon's waters flow.

II.

No guns are fired, no joy-bell rings:
  But neighbours call to see the boy
  And mother, and to wish them joy,
And then—attend to other things.

III.

Some years glide by—the boy is man;
  At school they thought him apt to learn;
  And now he goes from home to earn
His livelihood, as best he can.

IV.

He takes the stage; he writes a play;
   'Tis well received; he writes again;
   His name is known, and courtly men
Are glad to hear what he may say.

V.

For he flings wreaths of pearls abroad,
   Like shells or daisies idly strung;
   Nor sparing brain, nor pen, nor tongue,
Nor waiting until men applaud;

VI.

But, like a bird, a noble song
   He sings, as Genius teaches him—
   Regardless of the critic's whim—
Whether he think it right or wrong.

VII.

Great Nature's book he wisely reads:
   He solves the mystery of life,
   And cuts, with philosophic knife,
The tangled knot of human deeds.

VIII.

Man's passion—madness, hatred, guile,
Hope, mercy, friendship, honour, truth;
The griefs of age—the joys of youth;
The patriot's tear—the villain's smile;

IX.

The modest gem—the tinselled gaud,
Of noble worth or base pretence;
The glory bought at blood's expense;
The power gained by force or fraud—

X.

On these his sun of genius shone,
Making a wondrous photograph,
Till even critics ceased to laugh,
And owned the picture nobly done.

XI.

The chromatrope of woman's heart;
The words forgot with passion's breath;
The vanity that conquers death;
The feathery smile that wings a dart;

XII.

The gentle care that makes man blest ;
  The truth far more than jewels worth ;
  The love that makes a heaven of earth—
All these to him were manifest.

XIII.

He touches the historic page—
  The dead return to life again,
  And feel and speak like real men,
Hero or lover, king or sage.

XIV.

The realms of air, with potent wand,
  He enters boldly as a king ;
  And fays, that float on viewless wing,
Sing dreamy songs at his command !

XV.

And witches point, with palsied hand,
  And blast the air with hellish chime ;
  And ghosts revisit earth a time,
With messages from spirit-land !

XVI.

He calls, and what men fancied dumb,
    Hills, groves, and lakes, and brooks, and stones,
    Answer him in a thousand tones,
Till silence makes a joyous hum.

XVII.

In fine, he made "the world a stage,"
    And all upon it act their parts—
    By Nature's prompting and by Art's—
For Art is Nature taught by age.

XVIII.

And, singing thus, he passed his days—
    Not without honour, it is true—
    Yet hardly understood by few,
And these were slow in giving praise.

XIX.

And men had lived in mist so long,
    Some could not bear his blaze of light,
    But shut their eyes, and said 'twas night,
When it 'twas just the noon of song.

XX.

But when his soul shook off its clay,
  And hied, its labour done, to God,
  Throughout the land that he had trod,
'Twas felt " A King is dead to-day!"

XXI.

And now, when centuries have flown,
  Some shout, "Come, build a monument,
  For all arrears of poet-rent,"—
As if *he* needed brass or stone!

XXII.

O man! how oft thy acts have lied!
  Thou crushest those who strive to live,
  And makest poor pretence to give
Fame unto him thou can'st not hide.

XXIII.

And some are honoured, being dead,
  By those who coldly turned aside,
  And gave them, living, but their pride,
When they, perhaps, were needing bread!

XXIV.

Yet not to all such honour comes—
   Only a few bright names are known
   Of all the "simple, great ones gone"—
The most are only found on tombs.

XXV.

But one shall never pass away—
   His, who was born in Stratford town,
   When brave Queen Bess wore England's crown,
Three hundred years ago to-day!

SPRING.

I.

O grand, old Earth of God's and ours,
　Once more thou doffest winter's veil,
　Once more the budding trees and flowers
And birds' sweet music bid thee hail !

II.

Is it a time for joy or care,
　O Earth ?—a time to laugh or weep ?
　What myriads in thy bosom sleep,
And we shall soon lie sleeping there !

III.

O Earth ! 'tis hard to understand
　Why thou should'st thus thy children crave !
　For art thou not a mighty grave,
Though strewn with flowers by God's good hand ?

C*

IV.

Thou hearest not, amid thy mirth,
   Nor carest though thy children die,
   And senseless in thy bosom lie,
Cold and unthought of, cruel Earth !

V.

And yet, O Earth ! a little seed,
   Dropt by man's hand within thy heart,
   Thou makest great, and dost impart
To him again for every need !

VI.

O Earth ! if seed that man lets fall
   Into thy heart, thou givest thus
   Back thirty, sixty-fold to us,
Thou art not cruel, after all !

VII.

Nor dost thou, Earth, thy children crave ;
   'Tis God that sows them as His seed,
   And by and bye they shall be freed,
As beauteous flowers for him who gave.

VIII.

O gay, Spring Earth of God's and ours,—
  Nay, rather, thou and we are His,
  And sun and stars and all that is,—
We bid thee hail with birds and flowers !

IN MEMORIAM.

I.

Our days of happiness Time hurries by,
   As though in haste his envy found relief ;
But in our nights of anguish his cold eye
   Lingers upon us, gloating o'er our grief,—
Yet in the past we fain would live again,
Forgetting, for the gladness, all the pain.

II.

So pass our years.   It seems a little while
   Since, with wild throbbings in my boyish heart,
I westward gazed from my own western isle,
   And saw the white-winged messengers depart.
Ah ! little thought I then that o'er the sea
Lived any one that should be dear to me.

III.

Years fled—and other eyes were westward turned,
  And I was on the bosom of the deep,
While strange emotions in my bosom burned—
  A sorrow that I thought would never sleep :
For all that I had loved on earth was gone,—
Perhaps forever—and—I was alone ;

IV.

Save that I heard the dear familiar noise
  Of the old ocean, and can well recall
The bliss, the awe, the love without a voice
  With which I felt that great heart rise and fall,
Like some untamed and tameless " thing of life "
That frets for something worthy of its strife.

V.

And then I was alone amid the din
  Of ceaseless strugglers after wealth and power,
Content to hide the better soul within,
  And pass in men's applause a gaudy hour,—
To act out well a something they are not,—
To be admired and praised—despised, forgot.

VI.

I was alone, but in my fancy grew
  A fair ideal, fashioned from the best
And purest feelings that my spirit knew ;
  And this ideal was the goddess-guest
In my heart's temple ; but I sought not then
To find my goddess in the haunts of men.

VII.

And yet I found her—all-personified
  The goddess of my lonely-loving heart,
And—as an artist, when he stands beside
  Some genius-fathered, beauteous child of art,
Worships it mutely, with enraptured gaze—
My love was far too deep for words of praise.

VIII.

But, ah ! earth's brightest joys are bought with pain :
  Meeting with parting,—smiles with bitter tears,—
Hope ends in sorrow,—loss succeeds to gain,—
  And youth's gay spring-time leads to wintry years ;
Nought lives that dies not in the world's wide range,
And nothing is unchangeable but change.

IX.

My bliss was o'er. I was again alone
   Amid the scenes that I had learned to love
For her dear sake ; but, ah ! the charm was gone
   From river-side and mountain-slope and grove—
All, save the memory of happy hours
That lingered like the sweetness of dead flowers.

X.

And as the ground on which a temple stood
   Is holy, though the temple stand no more,
So river, mountain, waterfall and wood
   Wore something of the sacredness they wore
When her loved presence blessed them, and her face
Made all around her smile with her sweet grace.

XI.

And I am still alone, and years have fled,
   And other scenes are 'round me, as I call
The past by Memory's magic from the dead,
   As Endor's Sibyl brought the Seer to Saul.
(May *he* not then have thought of that good time
When David's music lulled his soul from crime?)

XII.

And I, with more of bitterness than bliss,
  The summoned years of my past life review,
Till Hope's red lips with love pale Sorrow's kiss,
  And all things good and beautiful and true,
Start rainbow-like from Sorrow's falling tears,
Spanning with hues of Heaven all my years.

XIII.

And as I ope the temple of my heart
  And seek its inmost and its holiest shrine,
Still there, my love, my darling one, thou art,—
  There still I worship thee and call thee mine ;
And this sweet anthem all that temple fills—
" Love cannot lose, 'tis loss of love that kills."

[POSTSCRIPT.]

XIV.

What cry was that which woke me from my dream ?
  I stand upon my native, island shore,
And hear the startled curlews round me scream
  O'er the mute cliffs that make the fierce waves roar ;
I watch the " stately ships " go sailing by,
And wonder how my heart has learned to sigh.

XV.

Ah ! *that* was but a dream.   A summer's eve
  Breathes all its balmy blessings on my brow ;
I feel as though the earth had got reprieve
  From its death-sentence.   See, the sun sets now—
The blue of heaven grows gently dark above,—
Below, blue eyes are growing dark with love.

XVI.

That, too, was but a dream.   What startled me ?
  The winds are making havoc 'mong the leaves
Of summer-time, and each once happy tree
  For its lost darlings rocks itself and grieves.
The night is dark, the sky is thick with clouds—
Kind frost-nymphs make the little leaves their shrouds !

WINTER.

Now lies Adonis in Prosérpine's breast,
  Who o'er him spreads a mantle lily white,
And every dryad, with disordered vest,
  Teareth her hair for sorrow at the sight.
And ere he waketh, many an eye, now bright,
  Shall deaden; many a rosy cheek shall pale;
O'er many a fair, young head shall rise the wail
  Of those whom Death hath spoiled of their delight.
And, when, at touch of Spring, the winding sheet
  That wraps thee now, Adonis, melts to flowers,
To deck thee for thy Queen; and sunny Hours,
  Dancing around thee on their soft swift feet,
Sing "Wake, Adonis;" many a one shall weep
  For those that in the Earth's dark bosom sleep.

PER NOCTEM PLURIMA VOLVENS.

I.

When the weary sun has ended his journey and
    descended,
By his own bright, golden pathway, to his mansion
    in the west,
And the sentry stars have taken the sky he has
    forsaken,
To watch till he awaken, bright and smiling, from
    his rest;

II.

And the Moon is rising slowly with a light serene
    and holy,
The Queen of all the watchers, the sister of the Sun,
And hushed are all the noises from Earth's unnum-
    bered voices,
And the heart of sleep rejoices in the conquest he
    has won ;

III.

In the still, unbroken quiet, free from day's unceas-
    ing riot,
I love to call around me the friends of long before,
And to fill my vacant places with the well-remem-
    bered graces
Of dear, old familiar faces that may smile for me
    no more.

IV.

Some that shared my boyish pastime, as they seemed
    to me the last time
That I saw them, full of life and joy and hope that
    knew no bound,
But who now are sad and grieving, and have lost
    the gay believing
In the deeds of hope's achieving, or—are laid beneath
    the ground ;—

V.

Some, not merely friends for pleasure, but who
    cherished friendship's treasure
More than gold or worldly honour or gay fashion's
    fickle smile,

Who would neither scorn nor flatter, who spoke
  honestly, no matter
How the world might grin and chatter, loving truth
  and hating guile ;—

VI.

Some whose silvery hair seemed saintly, and whose
  eyes though shining faintly,
Shed a tender lustre o'er me that will light me till
  the grave
That with all men I inherit takes my body, and my
  spirit,
Trusting in my Savour's merit, has returned to God
  who gave ;—

VII.

One, whom I have lost forever, but whom I will
  still endeavour
To deserve, though undeserving to have passed before her eyes,
For I know that while I love her, what is best and
  purest of her
Near me, through my life shall hover, like an angel
  from the skies ;—

VIII.

These, by Fancy, great enchanter, called, into my
  presence enter,
When the Sun and Earth are sleeping and the Moon
  and Stars are bright,
And whatever past seemed pleasant I live over in
  the present,
And the cares of day are lessened by the magic of
  the night.

BALAAM.

While sleep had set its seal on many eyes,
Balaam, the Seer, was forth beneath the stars,
Whose beauty glimmered in Euphrates' stream,
Gemming the mournful willows' floating hair.
Behind him were the mountains of the east,
The dark-browed nurses of the blue-eyed founts,
Whose lone hearts were the life of Pethor-land.
Westward, beyond the river, was the waste,
O'er which, this second time, with priceless gifts,
Had come from Balak noble messengers;
And westward were the eyes of Balaam turned,
As one who waits for one who does not come,
While wild things came and passed unheeded by,
And the night wind, as with an angel's harp,
Played lullaby to all the dreaming flowers.
And, gazing on the western sky, he saw
A picture, all whose forms were quick with life,
Where all was discord, hurrying to and fro,

As when two armies strive to gain the field;
For, from the outer realms of space, there came
Gigantic spearsmen, over whom there waved
Gay, many-coloured banners, and these flew,
Hither and thither, o'er the starry plain,
Pursuing and retreating; others came,
And others, till it seemed all Sabaoth
Had joined in conflict with the wicked one.
And then there was a change; banners and spears
Faded away, as fades away the reek
Above a hamlet on a frosty morn;
And none can tell when he sees last of it.
And, in a little while, there grew an arch,
Whose keystone was the zenith of the sky,
Like to a rainbow, joining east and west,
Beautiful, quivering, fearful, ominous,
Drawing the heart of Balaam after it.
And this, too, vanished, vapor-like, away;
And Balaam, though he waited its return,
Waited in vain; for warriors, and spears,
And banners, and the fiery flash of hosts
Embattled, and the mystic arch, were gone,
And came no more.

And Balaam stood amazed
Long time, while thoughts, conflicting, tore his breast,
And barred all passage for his voice.

        At length,
"Hath not the Highest, by this sign, declared
His purpose? I MUST GO!" he said, and then
Dark-boding terrors shook him and the strain
That held his face rapt westward, all relaxed
By speech, he felt as one, who, in a dream,
Stands on a steep cliff, by the greedy sea,
While ruthless foes pursue him.

        "I MUST GO!"
He said, and from ten thousand horrid throats
There seemed to come a mocking answer, "Go!"
And o'er him came a shiver, as a lake
Shivers beneath the burden of a breeze.
And then there came a whisper to his ear,
"Balaam, God's prophet! go not with these men!
Puttest thou Balak's honour above His
Who chose thee to declare His will to men?
Go, and thou art undone! God doth not lie!"
Then Balaam, as in answer to a friend:
"There came across the desert lordly men

D

From Moab and from Midian, who besought,
With many prayers and noble gifts, that I,
Balaam, the Seer, would go with them and curse
A people who were terrible in war—
To whom the strength of Moab was as grass
Before the oxen, feeding on the plains—
If, haply, I might crush them with a curse!
These prayed I to abide with me all night,
Till I should learn the purpose of the Lord—
And, in a dream, God warned me not to go;
And so they went away ungratified.
Then came these princes with more precious gifts,
And still more precious promises, who said,
'Balak, our lord, hath sent us unto thee,
And prayeth thee to come. He will promote
Thee and thy house to honour; and all boons,
Whate'er thou askest, he will freely give.'
And I replied, 'If Balak's house were full
Of gold and silver, and he made it mine,
Or more or less than God commandeth me,
I could not do. But tarry here to-night,
And I will hear the answer of the Lord.'
And then God sent a sign, the like of which

I, who know all the faces of the night,

And am familiar with all stars that shine

Over the hills and plains of Pethor-land,

Have never seen before, a sign which said:

'Balaam, if these men call thee, rise and go.'

Or more or less than God commandeth me

I cannot do.   Am I in this to blame?"

And then the wind came sweeping down the hills,

And Balaam heard again the mocking cry,

"If these man call thee, Balaam, rise and go."

And though he shuddered, all his face grew dark

And knotted, as he said, "God doth not lie,

But—doth God mock?   Hath he not sent a sign

To me, who have the power of reading signs,

His own high gift?   And now—and now, O God!

If thou wouldst send me yet another sign—!"

And here the whisper of the still, small voice

Came back, "O, Balaam! wretched is their fate,

Who, knowing good from evil, choose not good,

Or suffer evil, howsoever fair,

To make the good less lovely in their eyes!

Full well thou kowest that thy heart is set

More on the gold of Balak than God's will.

God doth not mock.   'Tis thou that mockest Him,
Coming into His presence, full of lust,
And seeking for a sign.   If thou wert pure
No sign were needed.   Being as thou art,
Wert thou to offer up the land's whole wealth,
Oxen and rams, and corn, and wine, and oil,
And all the first-born of thy kings, no sign
Would purge thee of those sordid dreams that drag
Thy soul from God to hell!

               It is not yet too late,
Perhaps, and but perhaps!

                  O, Balaam, rouse thee!
Thou art, e'en yet, God's prophet!   He has shewn
His will to none more clearly than to thee.
What is it He requireth at thy hands?
Be true and honest, pure and merciful,
Having thy heart aflame with faith and love,
Still walking humbly, as though prone to fall—
Guarding thine eyes from covetous wanderings,
Deeming God's gifts more beautiful than man's—
And he will keep thee right in all thy ways.
Oh! what is Balak's honour, Balak's gold,
To Balaam, if the Highest be his friend,

Who owns the wealth and beauty of the world?
Balaam, if these men call thee, do not go."
And Balaam bowed himself unto the ground,
And lay upon his face in misery;
And in his heart an awful battle raged,
Where evil fought with good. Longtime he lay,
As one entranced, all motionless, but full,
Through every nerve, of wakeful, painful life.
And then he rose, as from his grave, so pale
And wild his visage; and he looked again,
Along the waste, towards the western sky,
But saw no sign, save that the stars grew dim,
And some were gone; and, even as he looked,
He seemed to hear from all the waking earth,
Borne through the gloaming on the mountain wind,
The words he loved and longed for and yet loathed,
" Balaam, if these men call thee, rise and go."

And once again a shudder shook his frame;
And once again he bowed him to the earth,
And lay upon his face in misery,
Until, from weariness, he fell asleep.

And as he slept, he dreamed he was 'a child

D*

And heard sweet music, soft as is the breeze
That steals through corn-fields on a summer's day,
And makes the flowers kiss sweetly, and the leaves
On every tree grow tremulous for joy.

And then there came a noble, swelling strain,
Like the grand chorus of victorious hosts
That still march on to victory ; and he heard,
And was a man, with men—a king of men,
With crown of inspiration on his brow.
Around him thronged the chiefs of Pethor-land
And others, from afar, who came to hear
The wisdom God had given to his lips.
But he was still as humble as the child
That played of yore amid the flowers, and drew
From their sweet breath the beauty of the good.
And as he spoke, they listened to his words
As to an angel's : for his words were wise,
Wiser than all the wisdom of the East.

Then came a discord, as a sound of waves
That dash against tall rocks, while drowning men
Try vainly to be heard.   And Balaam grew

Proud with the pride of vain and worldly men,
And thought within his heart how great he was,
Forgetting who had made him wise and great ;
And thought of all the homage and the gifts
Yielded to him by princes of all lands,
Till his heart turned to evil more than good.

Then came a sound of battle and wild cries,
The blare of trumpets, and the clash of swords,
And the fierce neigh of war-steeds, and the groans
Of dying men,—and Balaam lay with these,
Far from the hills and streams of Pethor-land.
And, as he lay, he heard an awful voice,
High o'er the din of battle, and the words,
" If these men call thee, Balaam, rise and go."
And Balaam woke ; and on the Eastern hills
Beheld the ruddy blossom of the day
Bursting from out the sapphire of the sky ;
And all the earth looked pure as when it rose,
At first, in beauty, from the primal sea,
And all the heavenly hosts sang songs of joy.

But still the night lingered in Balaam's soul,

And all the pleasant voices of the morn,
With which, erstwhile, he joined in hymns of praise,
Were buried, as all hues are lost in black,
In the dark horrors of one fatal cry,
" If these men call thee, Balaam, rise and go."

And fainter was the whisper than before,
And Balaam heard it not, or heeded not,
As with slow steps—as one who walks in chains—
And head bowed low upon his breast, he moved
Homeward to where the princes waited him.

And Balaam told them not of sign or dream,
But only made him ready for the road.
And ere the sun was half-way up the sky,
Both he and they were far upon the waste
That stretched towards Moab,—and he nevermore
Beheld the hills and streams of Pethor-land.

GOOD NIGHT.

I.

Good night! God bless thee, love, wherever thou
    art,
And keep thee, like an infant, in His arms!
And all good messengers that move unseen
By eye sin-darkened, and on noiseless wings
Carry glad tidings to the doors of sleep,
Touch all thy tears to pearls of heavenly joy.
    Oh! I am very lonely, missing thee;
Yet, morning, noon, and night, sweet memories
Are nestling round thy name within my heart,
Like summer birds in frozen winter woods.
    Good night! *Good night!* oh, for the mutual
    word!
Oh, for the loving pressure of thy hand!
Oh, for the tender parting of thine eyes!
God bless thee, love, wherever thou art! Good
    night.

II.

Good night, my love! Another day has brought
Its load of grief and stowed it in my heart,
So full already, Joy is crushed to death,
And Hope stands mute and shivering at the door.
Still Memory, kind angel, stays within,
And will not leave me with my grief alone,
But whispers of the happy days that were
Made glorious by the light of thy pure eyes.
    Oh! shall I ever see thee, love, again,
My own, my darling, my soul's best beloved,
Far more than I had ever hoped to find
Of true and good and beautiful on earth?
Oh! shall I *never* see thee, love, again?
My treasure found and loved and lost, good night.

III.

Good night, my love! Without, the wintry winds
Make the night sadly vocal; and within,
The hours that danced along so full of joy,
Like skeletons have come from out their graves,
And sit beside me at my lonely fire, --

Guests grim but welcome, which my fancy decks,

In all the beauty that was theirs when thou

Didst look and breathe and whisper softly on them.

So do they come and sit, night after night,

Talking to me of thee till I forget

That they are mere illusions and the past

Is gone forever. They have vanished now,

And I am all alone, and thou art—where?

My love, good angels bear thee my good night!

WINTER SUNSHINE.

The " Miserere " of the wintry earth
    Went up to Heaven on the wings of air—
I heard it, sitting by my lonely hearth—
    An awful music ; sighs and moans of prayer,
The anguish human words could never bear
    Into God's ear, the agony whose birth
The soul hides from itself were mingled there
    With the fierce undertones of frantic mirth.
Then came a hush, and suddenly the floor
    Was carpeted with sunshine, living gold,
That filled the heart with summer ; Heaven's door
    Was touched and opened, and at once there rolled,
In strains of sweetest music from above,
    Back to the earth an answer, " God is Love ! "

CHRISTUS SALVATOR.

I.

C horo sancto nunciatus,

H omo, Deus Increatus,

R egum, Rex, Puellâ natus,

I n ignaris habitat ;

S umit vilem carnis vestem,

T radens Gloriam Cœlestem

U t dispellat culpæ pestem,

S atanamque subigat.

II.

S urgit Stella prophetarum,

A dest Victor tenebrarum,

L umen omnium terrarum,

V ia, Vita, Veritas.

A nimas illuminavit,

T enebrarum vim fugavit,

O ras Cœlicas monstravit

R edemptoris Claritas.

CHRISTMAS, 1864.

E

DEW.

"Who hath begotten the drops of dew?"—JOB xxxviii, 28.

I.

Who hath begotten the drops of dew?
    Tell, if you can, the tale of their birth;
Have the stars from Heaven come down to woo
    The flowers, the beautiful daughters of earth?

II.

Who hath begotten the drops of dew?
    Have angels open'd the pearly doors,
And, leaving their streets of golden hue,
    Blest with their footsteps our grassy floors?

III.

Who hath begotten the drops of dew?
    Doth not each orb in its bosom bear
Ruby and topaz and sapphire blue,
    And all the colours that angels wear?

IV.

Who hath begotten the drops of dew?

    Are they the tears of the saints above,

Returned to visit the scenes they knew,

    And to weep and pray for some earthly love?

V.

Who hath begotten the drops of dew?

    Who, the good that in all things lies?

Who, the primal beauty that grew

    Into myriad forms in Paradise?

VI.

Who hath begotten the drops of dew?

    Tell, if you can, the tale of their birth;

Are they not, children of men, with you,

    Sons of the Lord of *Heaven* and *Earth?*

THALATTA! THALATTA!

I.

In my ear is the moan of the pines—in my heart
    is the song of the sea,
And I feel his salt breath on my face as he showers
    his kisses on me,
And I hear the wild scream of the gulls, as they
    answer the call of the tide,
And I watch the fair sails as they glisten like gems
    on the breast of a bride.

II.

From the rock where I stand to the sun is a path-
    way of sapphire and gold,
Like a waif of those Patmian visions that wrapt
    the lone seer of old,
And it seems to my soul like an omen that calls
    me far over the sea—
But I think of a little white cottage and one that
    is dearest to me.

III.

Westward ho! Far away to the East is a cottage
    that looks to the shore—
Though each drop in the sea were a tear, as it was,
    I can see it no more ;
For the heart of its pride with the flowers of the
    " Vale of the Shadow " reclines,
And—hushed is the song of the sea and hoarse is
    the moan of the pines.

RIZPAH.

(2 SAMUEL xxi. 10.)

It is growing dark.
At such a sunset I have been with Saul—
But saw it not. I only saw his eyes
And the wild beauty of his roaming locks,
And—Oh! there never was a man like Saul!
Strong arm, and gentle heart and tender ways
To win a woman's very soul, were his.
When he would take my hand and look on me,
And whisper "Rizpah"—Ah! those days are gone!
Why should I weep? was I not loved by Saul?
And Saul was king of all the Land of God.

"God save the king!" But, hush! what noise was
    that?
Oh heaven! to think a mother's eyes should look
On such a sight! Away! vile carrion-beast!
Those are the sons of Saul,—poor Rizpah's sons.

O my dead darlings! O my only joy!

O sweet twin treasure of my lonely life,

Since that most mournful day upon Gilboa,

Torn from me thus!

            I have no tears to shed.

O God! my heart is broken! Let me die!

   *   *   *   *   *   *

Gilboa! David wrote a song on it,

And had it put in *Jasher*—"Weep for Saul."

Armoni used to sing it to his harp.

Poor blackened lips! · · · · · ·

   · · · · · I wonder if they dream,

My pretty children. · · · · · ·

   · · · · · Come, Mephibosheth,

Here is your father; say "God save the king!"

The Gibeonites! Ah! that was long ago.

Why should they die for what they never did?

No; David never would consent to that!

   *   *   *   *   *   *

Whose son is he, this youth? Dost know him,

     Abner?

Ha, ha! they shout again "God save the king."

   *   *   *   *   *   *

Was I asleep? I came not here to sleep.

O poor old eyes, sorrow has made you weak.

My sons! No, nought has touched them. O, how
     cold!

Cold, cold! O stars of God, have pity on me,

Poor lonely woman! O my sons, Saul's sons!

Kind stars, watch with me; let no evil beast

Rend that dear flesh. O God of Israel,

Pardon my sins! My heart is broken!

NATALIE.

I.

Such a pretty, siren face
  Thine was, Natalie !
Such a merry, winning grace
  Drew my heart to thee,
In those distant, happy days
  When thy heart was free.

II.

Fearless then we gathered joy,
  Not a care had we,
Happier girl and happier boy
  Well there could not be ;
In our bliss was no alloy,
  Playmate, Natalie.

E*

III.

Time is cruel. Thou and I
    Parted, Natalie!
And thy kissed lips said " Good bye!
    Surely write to me."
Thou wast then too young to sigh,
    Little Natalie!

IV.

One day, after years had flown,
    Something came to me,
'Twas a portrait of my own
    Playmate, Natalie,—
Natalie,—but not my own,
    Never mine to be!

V.

There she sat, so lovely grown,
    Like a queen to see,—
There she sat—but not alone,—
    With her—who is he?
So my boyish dream has flown,
    Faithless Natalie!

VI.

In my heart there is a place
  Still for Natalie !
For the pretty, siren face,
  For the sweetly, winning ways,
That were dear to me,
  In those happy far-off days,
When her heart was free.

THE FENIAN RAID.

June, 1866.

I.

The breath of the south wind was laden with woe
As it moaned to the Northland " Prepare for the
   foe ! "
And the Northland was silent a moment, and then
There was hieing and arming and marching of men.

II.

To the front ! There's a struggle—the crisis is past !
The foemen are flying ! woe, woe to the last !
There's a hush, only stirred by the zephyr of peace,
Wafting thanks to the God who makes fighting to
   cease.

III.

But, oh! with the voice of that zephyr a cry
Strives up after justice that seemeth to fly
From the nations of earth.—O our God have regard
To that cry; let the cause of the injured be heard!

IV.

From the blood of the true, the unselfish, the brave,
From the women and children they perished to save,
Goes a cry that no sound of rejoicing can still:
" Judge between us and those who have sanctioned
      this ill."

Humanum est errare,
Divinum condonare.

'Tis easy to cry " Raca * " from within
    Cold, passionless morality's strong tower,
    To those who struggle fiercely, hour by hour,
'Gainst grim Goliaths of unconquered sin.

'Tis easy, safely far from battle's din,
    To wave a sword or raise a banner high
    To those who have to fight each inch, or—die ;
Who must be wounded, even if they win.

'Tis easy to point clean, weak hands of scorn
    When some much-tempted brother falls or flies ;
    Or some sweet Eve has strayed from Paradise
Into the outer world of briar and thorn.

But in the great, high council of the skies
There's One who reads men's hearts with milder eyes.

* St. Matthew's Gospel v. 22.

SING ME THE SONGS I LOVE.

Sing me the songs I love once more,
    The songs your lips have made so dear,
For many a day must pass before
    Again your music fills my ear.
And when you are no longer near,
    I'll in my loneliness rejoice,
Deep in my inmost heart, to hear
    The gentle music of your voice.

'Tis not in words that friendship lies,
    E'en when those words in music move,
But words have power that never dies,
    When said or sung by those we love.
So when in weariness I rove
    Through the world's desert, seeking rest,
The memory of your songs shall prove
    A solace to my lonely breast.

And when you sing those songs again,
 For gayer hearts and brighter eyes,
And thinking upon " now " as " *then*,"
 Memories of other days arise,
Believe that none more dearly prize
 The strains your lips so sweetly pour,
Than he who asked 'neath other skies,
  " Sing me the songs I love once more."

IN MEMORIAM.

He is dead ! and what words can we say that will
    tell half the sorrow we know ;
He is murdered ! and mutters for vengeance are
    mingled with wailings of woe ;
He is gone ! and the voice that thrilled thousands,
    like music, forever is hushed ;
He lies bleeding ! and with him the heart of the
    nation lies bleeding and crushed !

Ah ! yes, he is gone ! The pure stars that lighted
    him home to his rest,
Saw his blood as he lay there, a martyr, his hand
    to a motionless breast ;
And the wings of the angels that quivered a moment
    before with his words,
Flashed again—" He is dead," and the souls of the
    waking were pierced as with swords.

Hardly strange doth it seem that the Springtime
    refuseth this morn to be gay,
And covers her eyes with a veil, and putteth her
    garlands away,
For she feels that the heart of a prophet of man
    and of nature is still,
And she hideth her flowers in her bosom and can-
    not be gay, if she will !

O Canada, weep, 'twas for thee that he spoke the
    last words of his life !
Weep, Erin, his blood has been shed in the healing
    of wounds of thy strife !
Weep, Scotia, no son of thy soil held thy mountains
    and valleys more dear !
Weep, England, thy brave, honest eyes never glis-
    tened with worthier tear !

He was true to himself, to his faith, to the lands
    of his birth and his choice ;
He was true, when, a boy, he obeyed, as he deemed
    it, a patriot voice ;

He was true, as a man, to the light gained by years,
    spite of slanderous breath ;
He was true, as the champion of peace, amid foes,
    under ban, *unto death !*

" Had he faults?" men will ask. Who is faultless?
    How many there are who redeem
Not the faults that they have by one virtue to make
    them a shield of esteem,
But lie evermore all content in their grave of mis-
    doing ; but he
Sent a light through his life that makes glorious for
    ever the name of McGEE.

APRIL 7th, 1868.

KILLYNOOGAN.

I.

Killynoogan,—hallowed name,—
Though thou'rt little known to fame,
My heart's homage thou dost claim.

II.

Though to stranger ears thou be
But a word of mystery,
Meaning deep thou hast for me.

III.

All thy quaint old masonry
Now before my eyes I see,
As, of old, it used to be.

IV.

Ah! too well I can recall
Every stone in every wall,—
In my heart I count them all.

V.

And the lawn before the door,
I can see it as of yore,
Bright with daisies spangled o'er.

VI.

And the hedge, along whose side,
Oft, in childhood, I have tried
To escape, when playing " Hide."

VII.

And the miniature wood,
Where in boyhood I have sued
Coyish maiden, Solitude.

VIII.

And the garden full of flowers,
Where I've past romantic hours,
Dreaming of fair ladies' bowers.

IX.

In the orchard, stretched at ease,
On the grass, I hear the breeze
Piping 'mong the apple trees.

X.

While from many a leafy nook,
Grave as parson at his book,
Rook replieth unto rook.

XI.

I can hear the river's flow
As it murmurs, soft and low,
Bringing news from Pettigo.

XII.

I can watch it to the mill,
Where the never-tiring wheel
Dances round and drinks its fill.

XIII.

Past the ever-bubbling "spa,"
Past the castle of Magra,
Razed by Cromwell's cruel law,

XIV.

On it goes with many a turn,
Playing with its fringe of fern,
Till it touches broad Lough Erne.

XV.

Here I leave thee, little stream,
Lost, like much I dearest deem,
In my life's oft-shifting dream.

XVI.

Lost! but let me backward haste,
I have little time to waste
In my ramble through the past.

XVII.

Words are cumbersome, at times,
Thought could visit fifty climes,
While I'm seeking useless rhymes.

XVIII.

I am back upon the lawn,
That I've often stood upon,
But—is every body gone?

XIX.

Knock,—is any one within?
Not a sound, except the din
Of the mice,—they must be thin.

XX.

Look along the avenue,
Is there any one in view?
Surely, this cannòt be true?

XXI.

Put your ear upon the ground!
Listen! Is there any sound?
Every thing is hushed around.

XXII.

Oh! I dream! I might have known ;
I have wandered,—*they* are gone,
And of *four* remains but *one.*

XXIII.

Two were young and two were old ;
Three are lying stark and cold
In death's rigid, icy fold.

XXIV.

Dear old Killynoogan, thee,
Once so full of life and glee,
Lifeless, desolate, I see !

XXV.

But, beloved and sacred spot,
Nought of thee shall be forgot,
Till what I am now—is not.

F

" What can I do that others have not done?
   What can I think that others have not thought?
   What can I teach that others have not taught?
   What can I win that others have not won?
   What is there left for me beneath the sun?
   My labour seems so useless, all I try
   I weary of, before 'tis well begun ;
   I scorn to grovel and I cannot fly."

" Hush! hush! repining heart! there's One whose eye
   Esteems each honest thought and act and word
   Noble as poet's songs or patriot's sword.
   Be true to Him : He will not pass thee by.
   He may not ask thee 'mid His stars to shine,
   And yet He needeth thee ; His work is thine."

HASTINGS.

October 14th, 1066.

I.

October's woods are bright and gay, a thousand
colours vie
To win the golden smiles the Sun sends gleaming
thro' the sky ;
And tho' the flowers are dead and gone, one garden
seems the earth,
For, in God's world, as one charm dies, another
starts to birth.

II.

To every season is its own peculiar beauty given,
In every age of mortal men we see the Hand of
Heaven ;
And century to century utters a glorious speech,
And peace to war, and war to peace, eternal lessons
teach.

III.

O grand, old woods, your forest-sires were thus as
    bright and gay,
Before the axe's murderous voice had spoiled their
    sylvan play ;
When other axes smote our sires and laid them stiff
    and low,
On Hastings' unforgotten field, *eight hundred years ago.*

IV.

Eight hundred years ago, long years, before Jacques
    Cartier clomb
The Royal Height, where now no more the red men
    fearless roam !
Eight hundred years ago, long years before Colum-
    bus came
From stately Spain to find the world that ought to
    bear his name !

V.

The Sussex woods were bright and red on that
    October morn ;
And Sussex soil was red with blood before the next
    was born ;

But from that red united clay another race did
    start
On the great stage of destiny to act a noble part.

VI.

So God doth mould, as pleaseth Him, the nations
    of His choice ;
Now, in the battle-cry is heard His purifying voice ;
And now with Orphic strains of peace he draws to
    nationhood
The scattered tribes that dwell apart by mountain,
    sea and wood.

VII.

He took the lonely, poet Celt and taught him Roman
    lore,
Then from the wealds of Saxony He brought the
    sons of Thor ;
Next from his craggy home the Dane came riding
    o'er the sea,
And last, came William with his bands of Norman
    chivalry.

F*

VIII.

And now as our young nationhood is struggling into
    birth,
God grant its infant pulse may beat with our fore-
    fathers' worth !
And as we gather into *one*, let us recall with pride
That we are of the blood of those who fought where
    Harold died.

October, 1866.

THE NAUGHTY BOY.

(From H. C. Andersen's Tales.)

A good old poet sat by his hearth,
    While the wind and rain were raging abroad;
And he thought of the poor who roamed thro' the earth
    Without a home or friend but God,
While he was as snug as he could desire,
Roasting his apples before the fire.

And just with the thought came a voice outside:
    "O pray, let me in, I am wet and cold."
In a second the door has been opened wide,
    And there standeth a boy with ringlets of gold.
"Come in, my boy, there is warmth for thee here;
Come in and take share of my frugal cheer."

So the boy came in, and in spite of the storm
 A cherub he seemed who had come from the skies,
With his curly locks and his graceful form,
 And the sparkling beauty that lit his eyes;
But the bow that he bore was so spoilt with the rain,
One would say he could never have used it again.

Then the good old poet nursed the boy,
 And dried him and warmed him and gave him
  wine,
And his heart grew glad, and the spirit of joy
 Frolicked and danced o'er his face divine;
"Light of heart thou seemest, and light of head,
Pray, what is thy name?" the old poet said.

"My name is Love; dost thou know me not?
 Look, yonder my bow and my arrows lie,
And I'd have you beware. I'm a capital shot."
 "But your bow is spoilt." "Never mind; I'll
  try."
And he bent his bow, and he aimed a dart,
And the good old poet was shot thro' the heart.

And he fell from his chair, and he wept full sore :
    " Is this my reward for my apples and wine?"
But the Naughty Boy could be seen no more ;
    He was forth again, for the night grew fine.
" Bah! I'll warn all the boys and the girls I know,
If they play with this Love, they'll have nothing
        but woe."

So the good old poet he did his best
    To make others beware of a fate like his ;
And he shewed them the arrow that pierced his
        breast :
    " Now you see what a terrible boy he is !"
But an archer, who's never two moment's the same,
Like Proteus, it's hard to keep clear of his aim !

ROSA.

Thou art gone, sweet love, to take thy rest,
Like a weary child on thy mother's breast;
And thou hearest not, in thy calm deep sleep,
The voices of those that around thee weep.

Thou art gone where the weary find a home,
Where sickness and sorrow can never come ;
A flower too fair for earthly skies,
Thou art gone to bloom in Paradise.

Thou art gone, and I hear not thy gladsome tone,
But my heart is still beating " *alone, alone,*"—
Yet often in dreams do I hear a strain
As of angels bearing thee back again.

Thou art gone, and the world may not miss thee long,
For thou didst not care for its idle throng ;
But this fond bosom, in silent woe,
Shall carry thine image wherever I go.

Thou art gone, thou art gone! Shall we meet no more
By the sandy hill or the winding shore?
Or watch as the crested billows rise,
And the frightened curlew startling cries?

Thou art gone, but oh! in that land of peace
Where sin, and sorrow and anguish cease,
Where all is happy and bright and fair,
My own sweet love, may I meet thee there?

MARCH, 1857.

JUBAL.

(Book of Genesis iv. 21.)

The Sun soon kissed to flowers, the blood-stained sod,
From which the voice of Abel cried to God,
And drove his murderer to the land of Nod ;

And smiling, kindly watched them day by day,
Till they, like Abel, died and passed away,
And other flowers grew bright above their clay.

While with impartial kindness, year by year,
He kissed from Cain's curs'd face the awful tear
That flowed when that dread voice appalled his ear.

Still as at night the silent woods are stirred
By the lone calling of some mateless bird,
Ever that voice in Cain's sad heart was heard.

But busy hands for good or bad are best
To still the aching voices of the breast,
And load the body with the soul's unrest.

So, tow'rds the Sun the City Enoch rose,
Beneath Cain's hands, as in the desert grows
A palm whose shade the tawny outcast knows.

The City Enoch! from the first-born named
Of the first-born of woman, son of blood!
Built long ere Babel's boastful tower was shamed,
Earth's lonely capital before the flood!

The City Enoch! here were sown and grew
The seeds of Art when Art and life were long;
Here Lamech turned his misery to song,
Hence Jabal journeyed, seeking pastures new!

Here man's soft hand made brass and iron yield
To cunning shapes and uses,—wondrous skill!
Tearing earth's iron heart with iron will,
To see what secrets in it lay concealed!

And here, O music, like a dream of heaven,
Thy subtle thrills did touch the wearied brain,
With raptured, passionate longing to regain
The bliss of having naught to be forgiven!

Let me in fancy see thee rise again
O city of the Wanderer, seldom sought!
City of that wise Jubal who first taught
The harp and organ to the sons of men!

That I may learn the secret of his might,
Who, leaving earth unto his brother's care,
Did gentle battle with the powers of air,
And made them his and ours by victor's right!

Adah, the first-beloved of Lamech's wives,
Bare him two sons. Jabal, the eldest-born,
Grew up to manhood, strong and bold and free;
And leaving Enoch, sought a boundless home,
Living in tents, a king amid his flocks,
Setting his throne where'er his subjects thrived,
Lord, or allowed vicegerent under God,
Unto the "cattle on a thousand hills."

But Jubal, wise and gentle, 'tis for thee
That we would raise to life the giant shades
That lived and loved, and sinned and wept and died
Ere Heaven's great tears had washed away the crime

That stained the beauty of the early earth;
And Enoch, mistress of primeval Art,
Lay, the dead mistress of a drownèd world.

What was thy year, thy month, thy day of birth,
That we may mark it in our Calendar,
"On this day, in a year before the Flood,
Jubal was born, Inventor of the Harp?"
Where shall we seek this knowledge? Of the stars?
'Tis said by some our hearts and brains depend
Upon the union in their mystic dance
They happen to be forming at the hour
When we are born. Then we shall ask the stars.
For they may recollect the year and hour
They formed that wondrous figure when the power
Of music touched the soul of man
For the first time, and if they can,
'Twas then that Jubal's life began!

  Sibyl-stars, that sing the chorus
  Of the life that lies before us
  As we open mortal eyes!

Strange phrenologists of Heaven,

That infuse the spirit-leaven

Into nascent, infant brains,

That can make them dull or wise,

Forging subtle mental chains

That must bind us until death,

As ye calmly glitter o'er us,

When we draw our primal breath!

Mixing qualities together,

Just according to the weather,

Just according to the season,

And the point of daily time,

Noon or even, night or morn,

That we happen to be born,

For some sage, sidereal reason,

Which some sophomores call " chance,"

Some the " force of circumstance!"

Tell, O fatal stars, sublime,

What the swelling of the chime

Into which you wove your dance,

What the day and what the hour,

Was so happy as to dower

Earth with Music's heavenly power!

Tell the day of Jubal's birth,
Day of Jubilee to earth.

Was the "music of the spheres"
Audible to mortal ears?
Did the winds of Heaven sing
Till the forests clapped their hands?
Did the ocean, heralding,
Bear the tidings to all lands,
Whispering, " Rejoice, rejoice,"
Till the earth, unprisoning
All her sounds, became a Voice?
As the soaring of his wing
When the distant eagle moves,
Wakes to life the silent groves,
At the coming of their king!
Sibyl-stars, was this the way
That Earth greeted Jubal's day?

In those far shadowy years before the Flood
Jubal was born, and this is all we know;
Born in the land where Cain, in solitude
And occupation sought to hide his woe

Born with a gift, well-used, of sin the foe,
A heaven-sent harbinger of promised good.

Oh! was not Adah happy in her boy?
Oh! who could tell the secret of her joy,
When, with a mother's love, she pierced the veil
That childhood draws round genius, lest it fail
In its high aim, by adulation fed,
And only feel the poison, when 'tis dead?

And Lamech, first of bards, whose kindred art
Would welcome her sweet sister, watched his son
As day by day he saw the promise start
Towards accomplishment. Yet neither one,
Father nor mother, knew as yet the prize
For which they waited with such anxious eyes.

They saw that he was not of common mould:
His quiet thoughtfulness, his pensive ways,
His listening oft as to a story told,
With side-turned head, and distant, earnest gaze,
Told of some god-like purpose in his brain,
Though what it was they asked themselves in vain.

So Jubal grew in those far, shadowy years
Before the Flood; and so the music grew
Within his soul. The common air to him
Was as a constant feast; its slightest touch
Was joy to which all other joy was pain.
The first sensations of his infancy
Were blent with it. His mother's tender sighs,—
Half sighs, half laughter,—as she looked on him,
Wondering what sort of man he should become,
Were like the breath of angels to his ear;
And when his father's mighty voice came forth,
Majestic, through its bearded doors, he hushed
The tremulous beatings of his heart to hear.
And when his brother Jabal went away,
And there were sounds of sorrow in his home,
(And he wept too, though hardly knowing why)
He treasured up the sounds as precious things,
Until they seemed a portion of his life.

So did he gather all the tones of love
And joy and grief, by strange instinctive power;
And by and by, how anger wounds the air,
And all the passions of the fallen heart

That Satan hissed into the ear of Eve,
He sadly learned ; and yet with balanced sense,
His great, high gift, he traced through all the tones
The woman struggling with her serpent-foe,
And desperate yearnings for lost innocence.

But most he joyed to listen to the words
Of happy children, respited a while,
From fearful looking to the day of death ;
And it was Jubal's chief delight to wed
Their gladsome voices with the Eden notes
To which the first sweet marriage-hymn was set—
The silver-throated wooing of the birds—
The trilling of the zephyr-courted leaves—
The merry-hearted laughter of the brooks—
The multitudinous hum of joyous life—
The weird lullaby that Nature sings
Unto the darlings fondled in her lap,
Loving but helpless, and their low response ;
And all the vocal charms of summer time,
That wrap the soul in dreamy, languid bliss.

All gentle sounds nestled within his heart,

But not alone (though these he loved the most)
Were gentle sounds the study of the boy.
The mournful requiem of the dying leaves,—
The piping gales that make the forest dance,—
The tempest's rage, to which the pine and oak
Are but as playthings to an angry child :
The rain, the whirlwind and the thundercrash,—
The mountain torrent, "the vexed ocean's roar,"—
The noisy lapping of the tongues of fire,—
The howl of hungry, ravenous beasts of prey,—
All that is sad or mad in Nature's voice,—
All that reminds us of the awful words
That pierced the fancied hiding place of sin,
Ere yet the curse descended,—these he knew.
For, in those giant days before the Flood,
Nature and man were ever face to face,
Till Art grew, Nature's image, in man's heart.

So Jubal revelled in all sweet, grand sounds,
A seeming spendthrift, but with miser craft,
Locking his airy jewels in the casket
Of lovingest remembrance,—till the boy
Dreamed himself into manhood.

                              Then there weighed
Upon his brain the burden of a thought,—
To bring to life the music that his soul
Had gathered from the music of the world,—
To make, by cunning union, every tone
Of its great voice obedient to his will.
And so he planned, awake, and, sleeping, dreamed
Of this, his one idea; till at last
'Neath his creative hand the "Harp" was born.
And then he planned again, for life was long
In those far, shadowy years before the Flood,
Until the "Organ," in its mighty heart,
Echoed the throbbings of the heart of man.

APOLLO DROPT A SEED OF SONG.

I.

Apollo dropt a seed of song
　　Into my heart one day,
And, smiling godlike, passed along
　　Upon his heavenly way.

II.

I saw him make his golden arc,
　　For many a weary day,
But still the little seedling, dark
　　Lay hid beneath the clay.

III.

But gentle eyes, one joyous hour,
　　Shone where my seedling lay,—
O Love, tend well thy little flower,
　　And let it not decay.

VOX DEI.

The beauteous pyramid of harmless flame
Spelled G O D for Moses; but the thundered law
Was needed for the wild, unruly crowd.

The awful test of swift-consuming fire
Alone shewed Baal false to Baal's friends;
The "still, small voice" touched lone Elijah's heart.

So God speaks variously to various men:
To some in nature's sternest parables;
To others, in the breath that woos the flowers,
Until they blush and pale, and blush again.

To *these* the Decalogue were just as true
If uttered on a summer Sabbath-day
In village church—to *those* there is no God,
Till fiery rain has scarred the face of earth.

THE OLD WAR-HORSE.

I.

He paweth no more in the field,
Where glitter the spear and the shield;
Nor heareth the thunder of war,
Nor smelleth the battle afar;
In his eyes is no glory of gleam,
And his strength is the strength of a dream.

II.

He never turned back from the sword,
When the pride of the land was his lord,
Yet his neck is bowed meekly—the brave
Can be meek, aye, as meek as a slave,—
And he works near the dark of his day,—
'Twas *his* pride (he was taught) to obey.

III.

In the gloaming of life his old eyes
May see visions of glory arise ;
Who knows but within his old heart
May thousands of memories start
Of the march and the drum and the fife,
Of the charge and the cry and the strife?

IV.

Who can tell?   But, hark! once again
He hears, as in whispers the strain
Of that long-ago hid in his blood ;
It comes nearer; he paweth the mud
Of the street, and his sinews rejoice,
And he hears not his slave-master's voice !

V.

Though his form no gay war-trappings deck,
The thunder returns to his neck ;
Ha! ha! he is free! for the sound
Of the trumpet his soul has unbound !
He is off! not a pause, till he comes
To the midst of the din of the drums.

VI.

He has taken his place, as of yore,
He is marching to battle once more;
They may mock him as haggard and thin,
They may laugh at the marks on his skin,
But naught recks he; the master he bore,
His name may well cover them o'er.

VII.

The music is hushed; the array
Of the soldiers has vanished away;
The old charger, poor fellow, elate
No longer, returns to his fate;
And the light of his eyes has burned low,
And his paces are feeble and slow.

*　　*　　*　　*　　*　　*

VIII.

He has heard his last call to parade
From the trumpet of death and obeyed;
And the brave soldier-steed from all harness is freed
   Evermore, and his sleep
   Is so placid and deep,
He needs fear no awakening. Rest to his shade!

*　　*　　*　　*　　*　　*

IX.

There are men, there are women who toil
At the mill or the mart or the soil,
Who wearily drudge day by day
Till the soul of them seems to decay ;
Only *seems*,—for within, after all,
There's a something that waits for its call.

X.

And if even the call never come
In this world of the deaf and the dumb,
When the Great Trumpet music shall fall
On the ears of the quick and the dead,
  They shall burst from their clay
  And hasten away
To their place in that host of which God is the Head.

ELOISE.

I.

I'll call thee Elöise. Such eyes as thine
    With fatal beauty marred
    The peace of Abelard,
And dimmed with human love the light divine
That lingers near Religion's holy shrine!

II.

O pitiless eyes, you burn unto my soul,
    Each one a living coal
From off Love's altar! Fall, O silken lashes,
And shade me, like a screen, from their control,
Ere all my warm delight be turned to ashes!

III.

Oh, no! I cannot bear the shade. Burn on,
    And let me slowly perish with sweet fire,
    Myself at once the victim and the pyre,—
I die of cold when that dear heat is gone.

WHEN THE SPRING-TIME COMES.

I.

"When the Spring-time comes"—
So we say in wintry hours ;
And we look upon the snow,
While we think upon the flowers.
And we gaze till hope's bright glory is kindled in
our eyes,
And earth becomes an Eden full of beauty and delight,
Where the air is far too happy to bear any weight of
sighs,
And myriad forms of gentle things bring gladness to
the sight.
And we wander through and through,
Past the fairest trees and flowers,
Till we find the friends we knew,
And link their hands in ours,
And then, in ecstacy of bliss, we seek the sweetest
bowers.

II.

" When the Spring-time comes "—
     But ah ! the snow is cold,
And Death is colder still,—
     Whom may he not enfold?
The glory in our eyes that shone is dimmed with
     bitter tears,
And our Eden-flowers have faded into nothingness
     again ;
And we wander sadly, darkly, through a labyrinth
     of years,
And we call for vanished faces, and act wildly in
     our pain.
          And then there comes a calm,
            And our sorrow grows less bold,
          As Nature's mighty psalm,
            O'er God's own mountain rolled,
Once heralded the still, small voice to that lone seer
     of old.

III.

" When the Spring-time comes "—
     Think we of griefs we know ;

Had we foreseen them long,
    Could we have stood the blow?
Then should we not be thankful for the mercy that
    conceals
The future, whether dark or bright, from our too
    curious eyes?
God knows what's best for all of us; He covers or
    reveals,
As it seemeth to him best, the ill that in our path-
    way lies.
    So let us journey on,
        Content in weal or woe
    To feel at least that One
    Smiles on us as we go,
Who in sublime humility once suffered here below.

IV.

"When the Spring-time comes"—
    Let us live well the hours,
God's spring within the heart
    Will wreathe them all with flowers.
And when the snow has fallen over hand and heart
    and brain,

Some few may say above our graves "Let us be
  like to them,
And though we may not see them when the Spring-
  time comes again,
We hold their memory more dear than gold or
  precious gem.
  And at the great Spring day,
    When melted are the powers
  That hide our souls in clay,
    As winter hides the flowers,
May we wreathe amaranths with them in Eden's
  choicest bowers."

HOPE.

She touched me in my sorrow ; I awoke.
Her kind hands broke the fetters of my grief;
The light of smiles shone round me, as she spoke :
"I come, my friend, to bring thee sweet relief.
Of those that minister, I am the chief,
To man's sick heart; I made the tears of Eve
Bright with the hues of Heaven, when loth to leave
The joys her disobedience made so brief.
I sailed with Noah o'er the buried earth,
I sat with Hagar by the new-found well,
I solaced Joseph in his lonely cell,
I filled sad David's soul with songs of mirth."
Much more she whispered, till my heart grew bright
And sorrow vanished, as at dawn, the night.

DOMINION DAY.

JULY, 1st, 1867.

I.

Our land is flushed with love ; through the wealth
    of her gay-hued tresses
  From his bright-red fingers the sun has been
    dropping his amorous fire,
And her eyes are gladly oppressed with the weight
    of his lips' caresses,
  And the zephyr-throbs of her bosom keep time
    with the voice of his lyre.

II.

'Tis the noon of the sweet, strong summer, the king
    of the months of the year,
  And the king of the year is crowning our Land
    with his glory of love,
And the King of all kings, in whose crown each gem
    is the light of a sphere,
  Looks smilingly down on our Land from the
    height of His heaven above.

III.

For to-day she breathes what to her is the first of
    a nation's breath,
  As she lies 'neath the gaze of the sun, as a bride,
    or a child new-born,
Lies with fair motionless limbs in the beautiful sem-
    blance of death,
  Yet awake with the joy of a bird that awakes with
    the whisper of morn.

IV.

And her soul is drinking the music that flows
    through the golden lyre,
  From the deeps of the woods and waters and
    wonderful hearts of men,
From the long-hushed songs of the forest, the wild,
    primeval choir,
  Till she feels the breath of the Spirit move over
    her face again.

I.

Of the shadowy distant ages,
    (This is the song they sing),
That scorn historic pages,
    When the Maple alone was king ;

When the bears were lords of creation,
    The beaver's the only trade,
And the greatest Confederation
    Was that which the wolves had made.

2.

And then, long ages after,
    How the first of the forest men,
With sounds of war and laughter,
    Invaded the wild beast's den ;
They tell of the axe's ringing,
    Of the camp-fire's savage glee,
Of the pipe of peace and the singing
    Under the maple tree.

3.

And how strange birds of ocean
    Came from the dawn of day,
And woke untold commotion,
    Where'er they winged their way ;
How pale-faced men and cruel
    Carried the sword and brand,
In search of gold and jewel,
    Into the red man's land.

II

4.

How, with the warriors, others
    Of gentle manners came,
Who called the red men brothers
    And told them of His Name,
Who came from the Great Spirit,
    To bless mankind and save;
And who, for man's demerit,
    Suffered the cross and grave.

5.

How still in spite of preaching
    Of brotherhood and peace,
It seemed that war's stern teaching
    Should never, never cease;
How blood was shed like water,
    How treaties were despised,
How massacre and slaughter
    Were night and day devised.

6.

How, in the course of seasons,
    Other strange ocean birds
Brought violence and treasons,
    And smooth, deceitful words;

And how the first pale-faces
      Fought with the last who came,
Until a war of races
      Set all the woods aflame.

7.

How valiant deeds and noble
      Shone out amid the night,
Illuming scenes of trouble,
      With Heaven's blessed light;
How oft, in human nature,
      Though wofully defaced,
Was seen some god-like feature—
      A flower in a waste;

8.

Till now, through God's good guiding,
      Those who as foemen strove,
With heart in heart confiding,
      As brothers join in love;
Till, from lake, sea and ocean,
      Mountain and woody dell,
Is heard, with glad emotion,
      Division's passing-bell.

V.

So she hears, not in words, but in spirit, the change-
 ful tale of the past,
 As she leans to the sun with veins that are blue
 like the blue of the sky,
Hears with a smile on her lips that the demon
 Division is cast
 Into the river of death, as a monster worthy to die.

VI.

And she hears many tongues of men, that are singing as one in her praise,
 Calling her, all, by one name, a name that is
 noble and old,
Singing a pœan of joy for the light of the gladdest
 of days,
 Making a noise of thanksgiving for union more
 precious than gold.

VII.

I.

Canada, Canada, land of the maple,
 Queen of the forest and river and lake,

Open thy soul to the voice of thy people,
    Close not thy heart to the music they make.
        Bells, chime out merrily,
        Trumpets, call cheerily,
Silence is vocal, and sleep is awake!

2.

Canada, Canada, land of the beaver,
    Labour and skill have their triumph to-day;
Oh! may the joy of it flow like a river,
    Wider and deeper as time flies away.
        Bells, chime out merrily,
        Trumpets, call cheerily,
Science and industry laugh and are gay.

3.

Canada, Canada, land of the snow-bird,
    Emblem of constancy change cannot kill,
Faith, that no strange cup has ever unsobered,
    Drinketh, to-day, from love's chalice her fill.
        Bells, chime out merrily,
        Trumpets, call cheerily,
Loyalty singeth and treason is still!

H*

4.

Canada, Canada, land of the bravest,
Sons of the war-path, and sons of the sea,
Land of no slave-lash, to-day thou enslavest
Millions of hearts with affection for thee.
Bells, chime out merrily,
Trumpets, call cheerily,
Let the sky ring with the shout of the free.

5.

Canada, Canada, land of the fairest,
Daughters of snow that is kissed by the sun,
Binding the charms of all lands that are rarest,
Like the bright cestus of Venus in one!
Bells, chime out merrily,
Trumpets, call cheerily,
A new reign of beauty on earth is begun!

VIII.

I.

The ocean has kissed her feet
With cool, soft lips that smile,
And his breath is wondrously sweet
With the odours of many an isle.

2.

He has many a grand old song
  Of his grand, old fearless kings ;
And the voice from his breast is strong,
  As he sings and laughs as he sings.

3.

Though often his heart is sad
  With the weight of the gray-haired days
That were once as light and as glad
  As the soul of a child that plays.

4.

But to-day at Canada's feet,
  He smiles, as when Venus was born,
And the breath from his lips is as sweet
  As the breath of wet flowers at morn.

IX.

1.

The mountains raise their faces
  Up to the face of God ;
They are fresh with balmy graces
  And with flowers their feet are shod.

2.

In their soul is a noise of gladness,
  Their veins swell out with song,—
With a feathery touch of sadness,
  Like a dream of forgotten wrong.

3.

They have set their song to the metre
  Of the bright-eyed summer days,
And our Land, to-day they greet her,
  With lips that are red with praise.

X.

1.

Lake is calling to lake
  With a ripply, musical sound,
As though half afraid to awake
  The storm from his sleep profound.

2

The hem of their garments is gay
  With gardens that look to the south;
And the smile of the dawn of to-day
  Has touched them on bosom and mouth.

XI.

The rivers have gladly embraced,

    And carry the joy of the lakes,

Past mountain and island and waste,

    To where the sea's laughter outbreaks.

XII.

And sea and lake and mountain,

    And man and beast and bird—

Our happy Land's life fountain—

    By one great voice are stirred.

        Bells chime out merrily,

        Trumpets call cheerily,

        Cannons boom lustily,

        Greet the glad day!

        Rose-wreath and fleur-de-lys,

        Shamrock and thistle be

        Joined to the maple tree

        Now and for aye!

XIII.

Let the shout of our joy to-day be borne through

    the pulse of the sea,

To the grand old lands of our fathers,—a token

    of loyalest love;

And may the winds bring back sweet words, O our
    Land, to thee—
    As, in the far old time, the peace-leaf came
        with the dove.

XIV.

And long, long ages hence, when the Land that we
    love so well
    Has clasped us all (as a mother clasps her
        babe) to her motherly bosom,
Those who shall walk on the dust of us, with pride
    in their Land shall tell,
    Holding the fruit in their grateful hands, of the
        birth of to-day, the blossom.

IN MY HEART.

I.

In my heart are many chambers through which I
    wander free ;
Some are furnished, some are empty, some are sombre,
    some are light ;
Some are open to all comers, and of some I keep
    the key,
And I enter in the stillness of the night.

II.

But there's one I never enter,—it is closed to even
    me !
Only once its door was opened, and it shut for ever-
    more ;
And though sounds of many voices gather round it,
    like the sea,
It is silent, ever silent, as the shore.

III.

In that chamber, long ago, my love's casket was
     concealed,
And the jewel that it sheltered I knew only one
     could win ;
And my soul foreboded sorrow, should that jewel be
     revealed,
And I almost hoped that none might enter in.

IV.

Yet day and night I lingered by that fatal chamber
     door,
Till—she came at last, my darling one, of all the
     earth my own ;
And she entered—and she vanished with my jewel,
     which she wore ;
And the door was closed—and I was left alone.

V.

She gave me back no jewel, but the spirit of her eyes
Shone with tenderness a moment, as she closed that
     chamber door,

And the memory of that moment is all I have to
  prize,—
But *that, at least,* is mine for evermore.

VI.

Was she conscious, when she took it, that the jewel
  was my love?
Did she think it but a bauble, she might wear or
  toss aside?
I know not, I accuse not, but I hope that it may
  prove
A blessing, though she spurn it in her pride.

S I S E R A .

JUDGES v., 28–30.

" Why comes he not ? why comes he not,
    My brave and noble son ?
Why comes he not with his warlike men,
    And the trophies his sword has won?
How slowly roll his chariot wheels !
    How weary is the day !
Pride of thy mother's lonely heart,
    Why dost thou still delay?

He comes not yet ! will he never come
    To gladden these heavy eyes,
That have watched and watched from morn till eve,
    And again till the sun did rise ?
Shall I greet no more his look of joy,
    Nor hear his manly voice ?
Why comes he not with the spoils of war,
    And the damsels of his choice ? "

Years rushed along in their ceaseless course,
   But Sisera came no more,
With his mighty men and his captive maids,
   As he oft had come before.
A woman's hand had done the deed
   That laid a hero low ;—
A woman's heart had felt the grief
   That childless mothers know.

COLUMBA SIBYLLA.

Ex mediis viridem surgentem ut lœta columba
Undis aspexit, post tempora tristia, terram,
Et levibus volitans folia alis carpsit olivæ,
Pacifera et rediit, libertatemque futuram
Navali inclusis in carcere significavit ;
Sic terram, lœtis, super œquora vasta, Columbus
Insequitur, ventis astrisque faventibus, alis ;
Inventam et terram placidis consevit olivis.

Aevorum super æquora parva columba Columbum
Inscia persequitur cum vaticinantibus alis !
Omina nomina sunt et Verbo facta reguntur,
Prœteritum nectitque futuro Aeterna Catena.

SUMMER IS DEAD.

I.

Summer is dead. Shall we weep or laugh,
As we gaze on the dead queen's epitaph
  Which Autumn has written in letters of gold :
" She was bright and beautiful, blithe and young,
And through grove and meadow she gaily sung,
As with careless footsteps she danced along
  To the grave, where she now lies cold ? "

II.

Shall we weep that her beauty from earth has gone?
Shall we weep for the friends that with her have flown?
Shall we weep for those that with her have died ?
For the man that has perished in manhood's pride?
For the maiden that never can be a bride?
  For the hearts that are left alone ?

III.

Shall we laugh as we stand at earth's palace-door,
With the faded crown that poor Summer wore,
    And placing it on her sister's brow,
Forget the face that once smiled beneath
That faded crown, and the flowery breath
That parted those lips now cold in death?
    For Autumn is monarch now.

IV.

Summer is dead. Shall we laugh or weep?
Is she really dead or only asleep
    With her sleeping garments on?
She only sleeps, and in meadow and grove
Again in gay dances her steps shall move;
But shall she come back with the friends we love?
    God knows, and His will be done.

ON A DEAD FIELD-FLOWER.

Torn by some careless hand
From thy mother's breast,
Where gentle breezes fann'd
Thy little leaves to rest,
Here dost thou lie, forsaken,
No more shalt thou awaken,
To gladden with thy beauty the wanderer opprest!

No more at early morn,
When the lark's gay song,
Through grove and meadow borne,
Calls his merry mates along,
Shall thy tiny arms, outspreading,
Their grateful odour shedding,
Give silent, speaking welcome to Nature's joyous
throng!

Peaceful and calm thy sleep!
Thy life's race run,
Thou hadst no cause to weep,
No duty left undone!
Sweet little withered blossom,
How many a blighted bosom
Would fain repose as softly beneath a summer's sun!

How many a child of care,
Won by thy power,
Might raise his voice in prayer,
Taught by thee, little flower!
Ah! surely thou wast given,
A gracious boon from heaven,
To throw its charm on sinful earth for one short
blissful hour!

Farewell! I may not stay;
Thy frail, drooping form
Heeds not the sun's fierce ray,
Nor winter's frowning storm!

Like thee, kind hearts have perish'd
By those that should have cherish'd,
And held the shield of friendship to shelter them
from harm.

Like thee, I soon must fade,
And 'neath the sky
Lifeless and cold be laid!
But though I claim no sigh,
Though no fond heart may miss me
When death's pale lips shall kiss me,
If my short life be pure as thine, I need not fear to
die.

MAY, 1857.

LINES

WRITTEN ON THE DEPARTURE OF THE PRINCE OF WALES
FROM PORTLAND, OCTOBER, 1860.

(*Set to Music by* F. BARNBY, Esq., *and sung at a Concert given in
honour of the Prince, in Montreal, November 9th,* 1860.)

I.

He stands alone upon the deck,
A prince without a peer,
He hears the cannon's farewell boom,
The loud and loyal cheer—
A prayer from true New England hearts,
Honest and brave and free,
That God would guide Old England's heir
Safe o'er the stormy sea.
He sees the sad, regretful gaze
That marks him as he goes,
And prays that God may never make
Such trusty friends his foes,

But that, as brothers in the cause
Of Liberty and Right,
Under the sacred flag of Truth
They ever may unite.

II.

He stands alone upon the deck,
Son of the noblest Queen
That ever placed a royal crown
Upon a brow serene.
For her sake did we welcome him,
Who owns an empire's love ;
But now we bless him for his own,—
God bless him from above !
He stands alone, a boy in years,
A "mighty one" by birth,
Crowned with a love that far excels
The brightest crowns of earth ;
Nor thinks he of the pomp and power
That wait his glad return,
But thoughts of manly tenderness
Deep in his bosom burn.

III.

He stands alone upon the deck,
Though thousands gaze on him,
He sees them not, for fond regret
Has made his blue eyes dim ;
His boyish lip is quivering,
And flushed his boyish cheek,
And his tearful eye speaks more, by far,
Than words could ever speak.
God grant that he may ever be
As good a prince as now,
Nor ever may true virtue's crown
Be lifted from his brow!
God bless him for his mother's sake,
God bless him for his own,
As thus he stands upon the deck,
'Mid thousands all alone!

ODE ON THE MARRIAGE OF THE PRINCE OF WALES.

MARCH 10th, 1863.

I.

Roses of England of every hue,
Your heads were lately bowed with the dew
Of sorrow for one that was good and true,
Through the length and breadth of your Island-
     garden,
Missing a hand that had cared for you!
    He sleeps in your midst, O Roses,
    The Roses he loved and knew,
    And blest was your sorrow, Roses,
    You gave unto worth its due!

II.

But, O Roses, smile again,
    He for whom you weep
Left his spirit among men
    When he fell asleep,—

Left his spirit and his name,
Left his pure, unspotted fame,
One who lives them all can claim.
Smile on him, O Roses!
He whose head reposes
In a sacred spot of your Island-garden,
Left him to you, good, brave and true,
To cherish and guard you, Roses!

III.

And now to you he brings
A treasure to keep and love,
From the north-land home of the old sea kings,—
A beautiful Danish Dove!
I heard proud Ocean's waves,
England's and Denmark's slaves,
Tell it in all the caves
That peep through the wall of your Island-garden!
Then welcome her sweetly, Roses,
She shall nestle among you soon,
And shall be to the loved of him whom you loved
In sorrow a priceless boon!

IV.

Winds that sport with the sea,
    Go east, west, south and north,
And from every Rose of the English tree
    That remembers its English birth
Carry from far and wide
    A gentle message of love
To the lone Rose-queen and her garden's
    pride,
    And his beautiful Danish Dove.

TO A SNOWBIRD.

I.

O gentle little comer
    In wintry days,
Far more than songs of summer
    I love thy lays.
They come when flowers are sweetest,
    And leaves are green ;
But thou thy song repeatest
    In sterner scene.

II.

In joyous days are many
    The friends we find ;
In dark ones scarcely any,
    To soothe the mind.
But friends in hours of sorrow
    Far more we prize
Than those that go to-morrow
    If storms arise.

THE CLOUDS ARE BLUSHING.

The clouds are blushing, the sun is gone,
He has been kissing them, every one,
Except the shy ones, that kept away,
And tearfully watched his parting ray ;
   But they love him no less
   For their bashfulness ;
The truest of lovers are not the most gay.

The snn is gone, and the blushing clouds
Are growing dimmer, as Night enshrouds
Sky, sea and land in her sombre pall—
The sexton at old Earth's funeral,
   When her race is run,
   And her work is done,
And her children are weaned from her, one and all.

The Man of the Moon has lit his lamp,
And is now commencing his airy tramp,

To see how the stars, those merry elves
That wink as he passes, behave themselves.

  With steady pace
  He is running his race,
Holding his lamp with a dignified grace.

The sun is rising behind the hill,
And I am waiting and watching still—
Waiting and watching, as night goes by,
What queer little scenes take place in the sky,

  When the silence is deep
  And men are asleep,
And none are awake but the stars and I !

MAY, 1859.

UNSPOKEN.

. . . . Quis prodere tanta relatu
. . . . possit ?
—Claudian.

There is a voice that never stirs the lips,—
Felt, but not heard ; that vibrates through the soul,—
A solemn music ; but no human speech
Can give that music to the ambient air.

The noblest poem poet ever wrote ;
The brighest picture artist ever drew ;
The loftiest music lyrist ever sung ;
The gentlest accents woman ever spoke,—
Are paraphrases of a felt original,
That lip, or pen, or pencil, cannot show
Unto the seeing eye or listening ear.
The thoughts we utter are but half themselves.
The poet knows this well. The artist knows
His hands bear not the burden of his thoughts

Upon the canvas. The musician knows
His soul must ever perish on his lips.
Even the eye,—"the window of the soul,"—
Though it may shed a light a little way,
Gives but a glimpse of that which burns within.

The sweet, unconscious tenderness of flowers ;
The boundless awe of star-encircled night ;
The tear that trickles down an old man's cheek ;
Ocean's loud pulse, that makes our own beat high ;
The vocal throb of a great multitude ;
The pause when we have heard and said " Farewell,"
And feel the pressure of a hand that's gone ;
The thought that we have wronged our truest friend,
When he is sleeping in the arms of Death ;
The silent, fathomless anguish that engulfs
Him who has found the precious power to love,
And sees that all he loves is torn from him ;
His dying moments who is void of hope ;
Jezebel ; Nero ; Judas ; any one
Of all the hideous things that crawled through life
In human form ;—what mortal could express

All that he feels in one or all of these,
Giving the very image of his thought?

Life, Death, Hell, Judgment, Resurrection, GOD—
Who can express their meaning?   Who can bound
Awe that is infinite in finite words?

Thus much of us must ever be concealed—
Spite of the high ambition to be born
Of what is noblest in us,—till His breath
Who woke the morning stars to sing their song,
Awakes our souls to fuller utterance.

JEPHTHAH.

JUDGES xi.

I.

Rejoice ye tribes of Israel, the Lord was on your
    side,
Your fierce and daring enemies have fallen in their
    pride.
In vain the heathen strove against Jehovah's awful
    word,
For Ammon's proud, presumptuous sons have perished
    by the sword.

II.

From Aroer to Minnith and to Abel's fertile plain
Of twenty noble cities the "mighty men" are slain;
Rejoice, thou son of Gilead, the Lord hath heard
    thy vow,—
Thy foes are crushed, thy father's sons before thy
    presence bow.

III.

It is an hour of triumph to the warrior and his
    band,
An hour of stern rejoicing to all the chosen land,
When the conqueror of Ammon, the valiant of his
    race,
Beholds once more, with well-earned joy, his long-
    lost native place.

IV.

But who is this advancing with gay attendant crowd?
O Jephthah! dost remember now the vow that thou
    hast vowed?
Why is thy face so ghastly pale? why sinks thy
    noble head?
Thy daughter's blood must now atone for all that
    thou hast shed!

V.

Honour and pomp and victory are all forgotten now,
And clouds of darkest anguish sweep across the
    father's brow.

He speaks—his words are words of death : he orders—
is obeyed—
And lonely mountains mourn the fate of Israel's
queenly maid.

VI.

Rejoice, ye tribes of Israel, the Lord was on your
side,
Your fierce presumptuous enemies have fallen in
their pride ?
But, Jephthah, thou art childless now, lift up thy
voice and weep !
No sound of wailing can disturb thy daughter's
dreamless sleep !

MAY, 1858.

DE PROFUNDIS.

I've seen the Ocean try to kiss the Moon,
Till the wild effort of his hopeless love
Tortured him into madness, and the roar
From his great throat was terrible to hear ;
And his vast bosom heaved such awful sighs
As made Earth tremble to her very bones,
And all her children cling to her for fear.
    And I have watched and seen a gentle change
Come over him, till, like a child, he lay,
That, disappointed, cries herself asleep,
And on her sorrow angels paint a dream
So happy that her face is one sweet smile.
So have I seen the love-tost Ocean smile
After his fury, till I almost hoped
That the gay Moon would never tempt him more.
    But ever his heart throbs at her approach,
And he awakes in all the strength of love,
And frets himself to madness, watching her.

J

And when, as I have sometimes seen, the Sun,
His mighty rival, struts before his eyes
With her he loves, and warmly looks on her,
Oh! how his heart is torn with jealousy!
Oh! how he froths and foams and moans and raves,
Till all his energy is lost in sleep,
From which his love will rouse him soon again!

So did I learn the Ocean's tale of love,
Watching him, day by day, for many years,
Hearing him often murmur in his sleep
Such sweet, sad murmurs, that I pitied him ;
And, like Electra, sat beside his bed
Till all the madness of his love awoke.

O Ocean! thou art like the human heart,
Which craves forever what it cannot have,
And, though a little it forget its strife
Of longing, only wakes to long again
For that which is no more accessible
Than is the Moon to thee! Yet, shouldst thou lie
Dull, sluggish, motionless, thy very life
Would grow corrupt, and from the stagnant mass

All things abominable would creep forth
To soil with slimy poison the fair Earth ;
And that alone which moves thee to thy heart
Can keep thee pure and bright and beautiful !

So, by the anguish of a hopeless love,—
So, by the madness born of mental pain,—
So, by the endless strife of joy and fear,—
So, by all suff .ings, tortures, agonies,—
So, by the powers that shake it to its depths,—
So, by the very loss of what it seeks,—
The heart is purified, and that which seems
Its death gives it a fresher, truer life.

LOCHLEVEN.

" We passed Lochleven, and saw the Castle on the Lake from which poor Queen Mary escaped."—*The Queen's Journal.*

I.

Sweet words of pity! Oh! if thou could'st rise,
　　Fair Queen, from out the darkness of the tomb,
And their old beauty light again thine eyes,
　　And thy persuasive lips no more be dumb,—
If thou, in all thy charms, should'st thus appear,
　　How thy full heart would throb!　With what
　　　　surprise
And rapture thou would't watch thy gentle peer,
　　By sad Lochleven, as, with tender sighs,
She mourned thy fate,—" Poor Mary wandered here."

II.

This vengeance Time hath brought thee; and thy foe,
　　Should she, too, rise with envy in her breast,

Would see thee throned with mercy in the best
  And purest heart that ever beat below
The purple of a Queen ; whose veins are warm
  With that same blood that gave the beauteous glow
To thine own cheeks. In her still lives the charm,
  For which, in spite of all, men worshipped thee,—
Refined by honour, truth and purity.

UNUS ABEST.

I.

A group of merry children played ;
The smiling sun to watch them stayed ;
A cloud came by with deadly shade ;

> " Unus abest."

II.

Bright faces glow 'mid dance and game ;
Hush ! some one named a well - known name ;
But dance and song go on the same ;

> " Unus abest."

III.

A father joins his children's mirth ;
A mother mourns an awful dearth ;
" Ashes to ashes, earth to earth ;"

> " Unus abest."

IV.

One sits before a lonely fire,
Watching the flame's unsteady spire
Wasting with suicidal ire ;

> " Unus abest."

V.

Thus, day by day, in house or street,
We miss some form we used to meet ;
Some human heart has ceased to beat ;

> " Unus abest."

VI.

The years pass on ; our hair is grey ;
A few years more we'll pass away,
Each leaving to his friends to say

> " Unus abest."

VII.

Then let us live that, when the call
Of the Great Trumpet wakes us all,
These words from God's high throne may fall :

> " NULLUS ABEST."

THE PRODIGAL'S RETURN.

(St. Luke's Gospel, xv. 17-32.)

I.

Long, my Father, have I wandered
　　From the home I loved of old,—
All Thy tender mercies squandered,
　　All Thy loving-kindness sold.

II.

I have sinned against Thy goodness,
　　Mocked Thy sorrow, scorned Thy love ;
Treated all Thy care with rudeness,
　　'Gainst Thy gentle Spirit strove.

III.

Far from Thy free, bounteous table,
　　I have fed on husks of sin ;
Wayward, thankless, and unstable,
　　Father, wilt Thou take me in ?

IV.

Take me, oh! in mercy take me,
  To Thy blessed home again,
And let no enticement shake me,—
  Satan's wiles nor wicked men.

V.

I am sinful, doubting, fearing—
  Thou canst banish all alarm ;
I am weak, and blind, and erring—
  Thou canst shield from every harm.

VI.

Look upon me, crushed and broken,
  Humble, contrite, at Thy feet.
Dost Thou know me ?   Hast Thou spoken ?
  " Hast Thou come Thy child to meet ! "

VII.

Lost and found !   Once dead, now living !
  Once an outcast, now a son !
Once despairing, now believing,—
  I my Father's house have won.

BALLYSHANNON, 1855.

IT IS THE QUIET HOUR.

It is the quiet hour, when weary Day
Whispers adieu in his dark Sister's ear,
And my lone soul is wandering away
To blissful scenes that are no longer near ;
And well-known faces seem to smile again,
And voices long unheard sound blithe and gay,
As, when, of yore, a happy, careless train,
We plucked the flowers that grew by life's young way.
Sweet flowers !—destined to a swift decay !
Bright faces !—that on earth have smiled your last !
Gay voices !—that have ceased to sing the lay
That rose spontaneous in the joyous past !
Memory's own stars amid my night of pain,
Shine out and tell me " Love is not in vain ! "

ESSAYS

IN

TRANSLATION.

HECTOR AND ANDROMACHE.

THE PARTING.

(Homer's Iliad vi. 369—503.*)*

Thus, having done his duty to his gods
And to his country, Hector sought his home,
Where Art and Nature vied in loveliness.
Love winged his feet ; his home he quickly found.
But her whom his soul loved he found not there,
Her of the snowy arms, Andromache :
For she, with infant child and well-robed nurse,
Unto a tower that faced the Grecian camp
Had gone to watch and weep.   So Hector paused
Upon the threshold, as he left the house,
And made enquiry of the household maids :
" Come now, handmaidens, answer me in truth,
Whither white-armed Andromache has gone,
To seek my sisters, or my brothers' wives,

L

Or to Athene's temple, where a crowd
Of matrons seek the bright-haired goddess' wrath
To turn to mercy by the strength of tears ? "
A trusty servant quickly made response :
" Hector, my lord, right willingly my lips
Shall answer truthfully thy eager quest,—
Not to thy sisters, nor thy brothers' wives,
Nor to Athene's temple, where a crowd
Of matrons seek the bright-haired goddess' wrath
To turn to mercy by the strength of tears,
Has gone Andromache ; but she has gone
Unto a lofty tower of Ilion
To watch the contest, for bad tidings came
Of Greeks victorious and of Trojans slain ;
And at this moment, like a frenzied one,
She rushes to the rampart, while, behind,
Her darling boy is carried by his nurse."

She ceased ; nor waited Hector long, but rushed
Forth from the house, along the very way
That he had come, through fair-built Troja's streets ;
Nor paused he till he reached the Scæan gate,
(Through which he meant to hie him to the plain).

But here Andromache of queenly dower,

His wife, the daughter of Eëtion,

Who dwelt erstwhile 'neath Placus' woody height,

In Thebe, ruling o'er Cilician men,

Came running till she met him in the way.

With her, the nurse, who to her bosom held

An innocent-hearted babe, their only son,

His father's joy, in beauty like a star,

Scamandrius named by Hector, but the host

Called him Astyanax, the City's King,

Honouring Hector chief defence of Troy.

And now he looked on him, and smiled a smile

That spake his heart more than a thousand words,

And called the tears into his mother's eyes.

She, clinging to her husband, grasped his hand,

And, sobbing " Hector," spoke to him these words:

" Ah ! love, thy bravery will be thy bane,

And, seeking glory, thou forgettest *him*

And me, ah ! hapless me when thou art gone !

Soon, soon, I know it, all the foes of Troy,

Rushing on thee at once, shall take thy life.

And, when I miss thee, it were better far

That I were laid beneath the ground : for I

Shall then have none to comfort me, not one,
But woes on woes, when thou hast left me, Hector!
No sire have I, nor gentle mother left,—
Him, as thou know'st, the proud Achilles slew,
And razed his fair-built city to the ground.
High-gated Thebe.   Yet he spoiled him not,
Although he slew him, but, with reverence,
Laid him in glittering arms upon the pyre,
And raised a mound in honour of his name,
Which the hill-nymphs garlanded round with elms,
The daughters of the ægis-bearing Zeus.
And my seven brothers, in one fatal day,
Entered the gloomy shades where Pluto reigns,
Slain by the ruthless hand that slew my sire,
As, in their native fields, they watched the herds
Of kine, slow-footed, and of snowy sheep.
Nor did my queenly mother long survive,
For, led a captive to the Grecian camp,
With other spoils, the victor sent her home,
For goodly ransom, only to be slain
By the sure shaft of huntress Artemis.
But thou art father, mother, brother, spouse,
My pride, my Hector !   Oh ! then, pity me !

Stay here and watch with me upon this tower,—
Stay, stay, my Hector, go not hence to make
Thy child an orphan and a widow me !
But set the forces by the Fig-tree Hill,
Where the chief risk of hostile entrance lies,
And where the wall is weakest.   At that point
Already have the bravest of our foes—
Idomeneus and either Ajax, Diomede,
And the two sons of Atreus—made assault,
Whether incited thither by some voice
Prophetic, or high hope of victory.
So stay, my Hector, they will need thee here."

Then valiant Hector, of quick-glancing helm,
Thus made reply : " Of all that thou hast said,
My own true wife, I feel, I know the truth,
But—could I bear the taunts of Trojan chiefs
And stately Trojan dames, if, coward-like,
I skulked from battle in my country's need ?
Nor does my spirit keep me from the fight,
For I have learned, brave-hearted, 'mid the first,
To draw my sword in Ilion's defence,
To struggle for the honour of my sire

And for my own. Although too well I know
The day shall come when sacred Troy must fall,
And Priam and his war-like hosts, who well
Can wield in fight the ashen-handled spear !
But not the woes of my brave countrymen,
Nor yet my mother's nor my kingly sire's,
Nor all my brethren's who shall bite the dust
'Neath bitter foes, touch me so much as thine,
When some one of the brass-mailed Greeks shall end
Thy days of freedom, leading thee away
In tears ; and, haply, in far Argos, thou
May'st tend another's loom or water draw
From Hyperea's or Messeis' fount,—
A slavish duty forced on thee by fate.
And some one, looking on thy tears, may say :
' *She* was the wife of Hector, who excelled
In fight among the chiefs that fought for Troy.'
And thy poor heart will ache with vain regret
For him whose strong right arm would keep thee free.
Then may his heaped-up grave keep Hector's eyes
From looking on thy sorrow and disgrace !"

So spake the noble Hector, and his arms

Extended to receive his son ; but *he*
Shrank, crying, to his well-robed nurse's breast,
Fearing the war-like presence of his sire,
His brazen armour and the horse-hair crest
Above his helmet nodding fearfully.
And Hector took the helmet off his head
And laid it down, all gleaming, on the ground ;
And then he kissed and dandled him, and prayed
To Zeus and all the gods on his behalf :
" O Zeus and all ye gods, I pray you, grant
That this, my son, may, as his sire, excel,
And may he truly be the City's King !
And may men say of him, as he returns
From war : ' He's braver than his father was.'
May he from war-like men take gory spoils,
And may his mother glory in his might ! "

Such was the warrior's prayer ; and in the arms
Of his dear wife he placed the little child.
She clasped the treasure to her fragrant breast,
Tearfully smiling. And her husband's soul
Was touched with pity, and he nursed her hand,
And called her by her name : " Andromache,

My love, fret not thyself too much for me !
No man descends to Hades ere his time,
And none whoe'er is born escapes his fate,
Whether his heart be cowardly or brave.
But, love, returning home, apply thyself
To household duties, and thy handmaidens
Despatch to theirs, the distaff and the loom.
For war must be the business of men,
And of all men that have been born in Troy,
This war has need of none so much as me."
Thus having spoken, noble Hector placed
The waving helmet on his head again.
And, silently, Andromache returned
(Oft looking back through her fast-gushing tears)
To the fair mansion of her warrior spouse.

And there, amid her handmaidens, she wept ;
And they wept, too, mourning their lord as dead,
While yet he lived : for, though he lived, they said
They knew that he would never more return,
Exulting in his prowess, from the war.

THE LAMENT OF ANDROMACHE FOR HECTOR.

(Homer's Iliad xxii. 437-515.)

But she whom he had loved, Andromache,
Knew not of Hector's death, for none had come
To tell her of his stay without the walls.
    She in the lofty palace sat retired
Within her chamber, working at the loom,—
Weaving a purple vest, with varied flowers
Embroidered.
        But, as she her fair-haired maids
Enjoined to place upon the blazing fire
The spacious caldron, that the soothing bath
Might be for Hector ready when he came
Home from the battle, knowing not that he,
Betrayed by blue-eyed Pallas, bleeding lay
Beneath Achilles' hand, she heard the sound
Of weeping and of wailing on the walls;
And her limbs trembled, and the shuttle fell
Upon the ground.
        Then cried she to her maids :
" Come, quickly, follow me, that we may see
What thing has happened, for I surely heard

L*

My mother's voice.   My heart within my breast
Bounds to my lips,—my knees are stiff with fear,—
And—oh ! I dread some ill to Priam's house.
Ah, me ! I fear me much, great Peleus' son
Has severed my brave Hector from the town,
And drives him to the plain ; and soon his life
Will be the forfeit of his manly rage.
Never would he abide amid the crowd,
But must be ever foremost in the war,—
In valour without peer."

                 She said, and flew
Forth from the palace, like a frenzied one,
With throbbing heart ; and her maids followed her.

    But when she reached the tower, amid the throng,
She stood upon the wall, and gazed around,
Until she saw her Hector dragged along
With foul dishonour by the prancing steeds
Towards the Grecian ships ; and, at the sight,
Night, as of death, darkened her tearful eyes.

    Swooning, she fell, and scattered in her fall
The ornaments that bound her captive hair,
Wondrous in beauty, band, and wreath, and veil,
And fillet, Golden Aphrodite's gift,

What day brave Hector led Andromache
Forth from her father's house, Eëtion.

Her sisters, who were nigh, with gentle care
Received her sinking form, and by her side
Waited in fear lest she should wake no more.

But when, at last, the parted life returned
And the full sense of misery, she wept
Among her kinsfolk, and, with choking sobs,
Called Hector's name :

           " Ah, wretched me ! my Hector,
Surely a cruel fate has followed us
Since we were born,—thou, in this city, Troy,
In Priam's palace,—I, in far-off Thebes,
Where Placus rears on high his woody crest,
The hapless daughter of a hapless king !
Oh ! would that I had never seen the sun !
For now to Pluto's dark and drear abode
Thou hast descended, leaving me alone,
A mournful widow in thy empty halls.

And he who was his hapless parents' pride,
Our infant son, shall see thy face no more,
Nor ever more delight thy loving eyes,
Since thine are closed in death.

                              Unhappy boy !
If even he escape the Grecian sword,
Travail and woes must be henceforth his lot,
And stranger hands shall reap his father's fields,—
The woful day of orphanage has made
His life all friendless and companionless,—
The constant prey of grief, upon his cheek
The tears shall never dry,—and he must beg
With suppliant mien bread from his father's guests,
Scarce heeded, or, if heeded, poorly fed.

    His pampered peer in age, whose ev'ry need
Both parents well supply, with cruel hands
Thrusting him from the feast, will rudely say :
' Away ! begone ! thy father feasts not here.'
    Then to his widowed mother, all in tears,
My boy will come, my sweet Astyanax,
Who, erstwhile, fondled on his father's knee,
Shared in the choicest titbits of the board ;
And when, at eve, his childish prattle ceased,
Lulled by his tender nurse, his little head
Reposed on downy pillow, and his cheek
Glowed with the silent pleasure of his heart.
    Now is he doomed to pain, his father gone,

Whose valour won his name Astyanax,
' The City's King,'—for Hector was of Troy,
Its gates and lofty walls, the chief defence.

And thou, my Hector, liest all unclad
Far from thy kin, beside the high-prowed ships,—
Of ravenous dogs and coiling worms the prey,—
While in thy desert halls neglected lie
The soft, fair garments that were wrought for thee,
Alas ! in vain, by hands that love had taught.

These now must only deck thy funeral pyre,
In mournful honour to thy cherished name—
The glory and the strength of fallen Troy."

Thus spake she 'mid her tears, and, all around,
The listening chorus of her maidens wept.

THE BEACON LIGHT ANNOUNCING THE FALL OF TROY AT ARGOS.

(From the Agamemnon of Æschylus, v. 255.)

CHORUS AND CLYTEMNESTRA.

CL.—Word of joy this morning brings
     From the bosom of the night,
    Higher joy than Hope's gay wings
     Circled in her farthest flight!
    Troy is taken, Troy is fallen
     By the victor Argive's might!

CH.—Troy has fallen dost thou tell me?
    Have I heard thy words aright?

CL.—Hearken! I repeat the words,—
    Troy is held by Grecian lords.

CH.—Ah! what gladness fills my heart,
    And my tears with rapture start!

CL.—Yes, thine eyes thy feeling shew.

CH.—This by what proof dost thou know?

CL.—The gods, that never would deceive,
    Brought these tidings.

CH. —   Dost believe
    In the fickle shapes of dreams?

CL.—Nay; the dozings of the mind
    Leave in me no trace behind.

CH.—Some wild rumour, then, meseems?

CL.—Dost thou think me but a child,
    Thus and thus to be beguiled?

CH.—How long, then, is it since proud Ilion fell?

CL.—Since but the night that bore this morning's
    light.

CH.—And who this message hither brought so well?

Cl.—Hephæstus, sending forth his beacon bright
From Ida's summit; then, from height to height
With blaze successive, beacon kindling beacon,
Bore us the tidings.   Ida glanced it forth
To Lemnos, even to th' Hermæan rock ;
And next steep Athos, dear to Zeus, received
From Lemnos the bright flame, which, in its
    strength
Joyous, pursued its onward course, and flew
O'er the broad shoulders of Oceanus,
Giving its gleams all-golden, like the sun,
To those that on Makistos kept high watch.
Nor dallying he, nor won by ill-timed sleep,
Assumed his part of messenger ; and far
Over Euripus speeds the signal flame,
Telling their tasks to the Messapian guards,
Who answered with a blaze that straightway lit
The heather on old Graia's mountain-tops.
Then in full-gleaming strength, like a fair moon,
The beacon-light shot o'er Asopus plain,
And lit with answering fire Cithæron's cliff,
Whose emulous watch made brighter still the
    blaze.

Thence darted on the fiery messenger

Over Gorgopis lake and up the sides

Of Ægiplanctus, whence (the waiting wards

Heaping no niggard pile), a beard-like flame

Streamed onward till it touched the cliff that
    spies

The billows of the blue Saronic sea ;

But paused not in its course, until it reached

The heights of Arachnæum, over there.

And thence it strikes upon these palace-roofs,—

Far offspring of the light of fallen Troy.

PRIAM AND HELEN.

(*Iliad* iii. 161.)

Priam, the King, to the tower where he sat called
the beautiful Helen:

"Hither, my daughter, approach and sit by me here
on this tower,

Whence thou mayest see the spouse of thy youth, thy
friends and thy kindred.

Thou knowest I never blamed thee; I blame the
gods of Olympus,

Who excited this war of sorrows and tears without
number.

Come, Helen, sit by my side, and tell me the name
of yon hero,

Mighty and stately in mien. Though others around
him are taller,

One of such beauty as his and of so majestic a
bearing

I have never beheld. If he is not a king he is
kingly."

Then Helen, fairest of women, answered the King:
"O my father,
Father of Paris, by me thou art loved and revered
and respected!
Would that an evil death had been my lot when I
followed
Hither thy son, Alexander, leaving my husband
behind me,
Kinsmen, too, and sweet daughter, and friends that
I knew since my childhood!
'Twas not allowed me to die—so I pine away slowly
with weeping.
But thou awaitest reply: thou seest the great
Agamemnon,
Wide-ruling king, as thou saidst, and a warrior valiant
and skilful;
Once he was a brother to me—oh, shame!—in the
days that have vanished!"

Then, as a hero a hero, the old man admired
Agamemnon:
"Happy art thou, Atrides, in birth, and in name, and
in fortune;

Many are under thy sway—the flower of the sons
    of Achæa.

Once into vine-bearing Phrygia I entered, and saw
    many Phrygians

Riding swift steeds, the forces of Otreus and Mygdon,
    the godlike,

Who, with me for an ally, encamped by the banks of
    the Sangar,

Waiting the march of their foes, the Amazons,
    warrior-women :

But few in number were they to those quick-eyed
    sons of Achæa."

Next, perceiving Ulysses, the old man said, " My
    dear Helen,

Tell me who this is also—in stature less than
    Atrides,

Less by a head, it may be, but broader in chest and
    in shoulders.

Rest on the ground his arms ; but he through the
    ranks of the army

Ranges about like a ram ; to a thick-fleeced ram I
    compare him,

Wandering hither and thither through snow-white
    sheep in the pasture?"

Him then answered Helen—Helen of Jove descended:
"That is Ulysses, my father, the wily son of
    Laertes,
Nourished in Ithaca's isle — Ithaca rocky and
    barren ;
Skilled to contrive and complete wise plans and
    politic counsels."

Her then the sage Antenor addressed, when she
    spake of Ulysses:
"Lady, in truth thou hast uttered these words ; for
    once, I remember,
Hither the noble Ulysses came with the brave
    Menelaus,
(Thou wast the cause of his coming) and I was their
    host in my palace,
And of both the heroes I learned the genius and
    wisdom.
When they met in the Council, with Trojan heroes
    assembled,

Standing, Ulysses was less by a head than the
    brave Menelaus—

Sitting, more honour was due to the thoughtful
    brow of Ulysses.

And when they wove, for the general ear, their
    thoughts into language,

Menelaus harangued very freely and briefly, and clearly,

Never missing his words, nor misapplying their
    meaning,

Though, as to years, not yet was he reckoned
    among the elders.

But when Ulysses arose, with his head full of
    wariest measures,

Standing, he fixed his eyes on the ground, and kept
    looking downwards,

Moving his sceptre nor backwards nor forwards, but
    holding it firmly,

Looking like one not wise ; and those who beheld
    him might fancy

That he was deeply enraged, and thus bereft of his
    reason.

But when, as I have seen, he sent his great voice
    from his bosom,

Words that came thick and fast, like the flakes of
    the snow in the winter,
Then he that listened would say, no man might
    compete with Ulysse;
Then we forgot how he looked as the words of
    Ulysses enchained us."

Thirdly, on seeing Ajax, the old King of Helen
    demanded:
"Who, so stately and tall, is this other chief of the
    Grecians,
Rising as high o'er the rest as the height of his
    head and broad shoulders?"

And thus the comely-robed Helen, the fairest of
    women, responded:
"He thou beholdest is Ajax, gigantic—to Grecians
    a bulwark!
And over there, like a god, Idomeneus stands 'mong
    the Cretans,
While around him the chiefs of the Cretan army are
    gathered.
Many a time has the brave Menelaus bidden him
    welcome,

When to our Spartan home he came from the land
    of the Cretans.

But while I see all around, the rest of the dark-
    eyed Achæans,
Whom I well know, and whose names I could tell,
    two captains I see not—
Castor, tamer of steeds, and Pollux, skilful in
    boxing—
Both own brothers of mine : we three were nursed
    by one mother.
Either they have not come with the forces from far
    Lacedæmon,
Or having come, it may be, to this place, in sea-
    traversing vessels,
Do not desire, after all to enter the battle of
    heroes,
Fearing the shame and reproach the crime of their
    sister would cause them."

So she spake ; but them the life-giving earth was
    embracing
In the dear land of their fathers over the
    sea, Lacedæmon !

SONG OF THE TROJAN CAPTIVE.

(Euripidis Hecuba, 905.)

I.

O my Ilion, once we named thee
    City of unconquered men ;
But the Grecian spear has tamed thee,
    Thou canst never rise again.
Grecian clouds thy causeways darken ;—
    Ah ! they cannot hide thy glory !
Ages hence shall heroes hearken
    To the wonders of thy story.

II.

O my Ilion, they have shorn thee
    Of thy lofty crown of towers !
Thy poor daughter can but mourn thee
    In her lonely, captive hours.

M

They have robbed thee of thy beauty,
  Made thee foul with smoke and gore ;
Tears are now my only duty,
  I shall tread thy streets no more.

III.

O my Ilion, I remember—
  'Twas the hour of sweet repose,
And my husband in our chamber
  Slept, nor dreamt of Grecian foes.
For the song and feast were over,
  And the spear was hung to rest—
Never more, my hero-lover,
  Aimed by thee at foeman's breast.

IV.

O my Ilion, at the mirror
  I was binding up my hair,
When my face grew pale with terror
  At the cry that rent the air.
Hark ! amid the din, the Grecian
  Shout of triumph "Troy is taken ;
Ten years' work have now completion—
  Ilion's haughty towers are shaken !"

V.

O my Ilion, forth I hied me
    From his happy home and mine ;
Hapless, soon the Greeks descried me,
    As I knelt at Phœbe's shrine.
Then, my husband slain before me,
    To the shore they hurried me,
And from all I loved they tore me
    Fainting o'er the cruel sea.

BELLEROPHON.

(Iliad vi. 152—195.)

In a far nook of steed-famed Argos, stand
The city Ephyra. Here Sisyphus,
The wily son of Æolus, was king.

His son was Glaucus, and to him was born
Bellerophon of honour without stain,
Gifted with every grace the gods bestow,
And manly spirit that won all men's love.

Him Prœtus, who by Jove's supreme consent
Held a harsh sceptre over Argolis,
Hated and doomed to exile or to death.
For fair Antea loved Bellerophon
With a mad passion, and, her royal spouse
Deceiving, told her longing to his guest.
But brave Bellerophon, as good as brave,
Set a pure heart against her evil words.

Then with false tongue she stood before the king :
"O Prœtus, die or slay Bellerophon,
Who sought her love, who only loveth thee."
And anger seized the king at what he heard,
Yet was he loath to kill him, for the laws
That make the stranger sacred he revered.
But unto Lycia, bearing fatal signs,
And folded in a tablet, words of death,
He sent him, and enjoined him these to give
Unto Antea's sire—his step-father,
Thinking that he would perish.

                                    So he went,
Blameless, beneath the guidance of the gods,
And reached the eddying Xanthus. There the king
Of wide-extending Lycia honoured him
Nine days with feasting and with sacrifice.
But when the tenth rose-fingered morn had come,
He asked him for his message and the sign
Whate'er he bore from Prœtus,—which he gave.

And when he broke the evil-boding seal,
He first enjoined him the Chimæra dire

M*

To slay,—of race divine and not of men,
In front a lion, dragon in the rear,
And goat between, whose breath was as the strength
Of fiercely blazing fire.   And this he slew,
Trusting the portents of the gods.   And next
He conquered the wild, far-famed Solymi,—
The hardest battle fought with mortal men.
The man-like Amazons he next subdued;
And as he journed homeward, fearing nought,
An ambuscade of Lycia's bravest men,
Attacked him, but he slew them one by one,
And they returned no more.

                          And so the king
Seeing his race divine by noble deeds
Well proven, made the Lycian realm his home,
His beauteous daughter gave him for his wife,
And made him partner in his royal power.
And of the choicest land for corn and wine,
The Lycians gave him to possess and till.

HORACE.

(Book i. *Ode* xi.*)*

Seek not to know (for 'tis as wrong as vain)
    What term of life to thee or me
    The gods may grant, Leuconoe,
Nor with Chaldean numbers vex thy brain.
But calmly take what comes of joy or pain,
Whether Jove grant us many winters more,
    Or this complete our destiny
    Which makes the stormy Tuscan sea
    Weary its strength with angry shocks
    Against the hollow-echoing rocks.
Be gently wise, my friend, and while you pour
The ruddy wine, live long by living well.
While we are speaking, hark! time's envious knell!
    Let us enjoy to-day, nor borrow
    Vague grief by thinking of to.morrow.

ORPHEUS AND EURYDICE.

(From VIRGIL—*Georgic* IV. 457-527.*)*

The fair, young bride of Orpheus, as she fled
From Aristæus who designed her ill,
With hasty feet, along the river bank
Of Hebrus, found her death. For in her way
There lurked a baleful serpent 'mid the grass.

Full long the choir of Dryads mourned her fate,
And set the mountains wailing with their woe.
Pangæus answered back to Rhodope, and grief
Held all the land of Rhesus, dear to Mars ;
And Hebrus, weeping, rolled to distant shores
The story of the dead Eurydice.

But Orpheus in his sorrow touched his harp,
And, sitting by the wild beach all alone,
Sang from the rising till the setting sun
Of his own sweet, lost wife Eurydice.

Till, drawing solace to his wounded love,
Through the fierce jaws of Tænarus he passed,
The gates of Hades, and the gloomy grove,
All thick with darkest horror, and, at last,
Entered the drear abodes where Pluto reigns
Among the dead—inexorable king.

And then he put his fingers to the strings
And sang of her he loved, Eurydice ;
And made such sweet, enchanting melody
That all the ghosts of Erebus were charmed,
And hied from all recesses at the sound ;
Gathering around him, many as the birds
That hide themselves by thousands 'mid the leaves
Of some sweet-smelling grove, when eventide
Or wintry shower calls them from the hills.

The shades of mothers, sires and mighty men,
Of maids for whom the torch was never lit,
And boys whose pyres their parents' eyes had seen,
Listened, enchained, and for a while forgot
The slimy weeds that grew upon the banks,
Of black Cocytus, and the hateful Styx,
Whose nine slow streams shut out the happy world.

And even Tartarus, Death's deepest home,
Was stricken with amazement; and the rage
Of snake-tressed Furies ceased ; and Cerberus
Restrained his triple roar, and hellish blasts
Forbore a while to turn Ixion's wheel.

And now, all danger past, to upper air
He turned his eager feet, Eurydice
Restored, near-following (for Proserpine
Had so enjoined), when Orpheus, mad with joy
And longing to behold her face once more,
Paused and looked back, unmindful. Fatal look,
That robbed him of his treasure on the verge
Of full fruition in the world's broad light!
No hope of mercy ; Hell no mercy knows
For broken law. This Orpheus learned too late,
When triple thunder bellowed through the deeps
Of dark Avernus.

Then Eurydice :
"What frenzy, Orpheus, has possessed thy soul
To ruin thee and me, ah ! wretched me,
Whom now the Fates call back to Hades' gloom !

Alas! the sleep of death is on my eyes.

Farewell, my Orpheus! darkness hems me round—

Farewell! in vain I stretch weak hands to thee—

Thine, thine no more! Farewell! Farewell!"

                       She said,

And vanished from his sight away, as smoke

Fades into viewless air, nor saw she more

Her Orpheus.

        He in vain the fleeting shade

Sought to restrain with outspread hands; in vain

Essayed to speak, dumb-stricken with surprise;

In vain, to cross the gloomy Stygian wave.

Alas! what could he do, or whither go,

Since she was gone, the sum of all his joy?

Or, with what tears, what plaintive, moving words,

Seek respite from the gods that rule below

For her who, shivering, crossed the darksome stream?

So passed she from him; and, for seven long months

Beneath a rock by Strymon's lonely flood

He wailed her fate and his, till all the caves

Re-echoed mournfully, and savage beasts,

Assuaged, knew milder breasts, and strength of oaks

Was captive led by magic of his song.

Even as, in woods, beneath a poplar's shade

Lone Philomel laments her callow brood,

Robbed from the nest by cruel, churlish hands;

And she, poor childless mother, all night long,

Perched on a branch, renews the doleful strain,

And with her plaints makes all the grove resound;

So Orpheus mourned Eurydice, nor dreamed

Of other love, nor other nuptial tie.

Alone, 'mid Boreal ice, and by the banks

Of snow-girt Tanais, and through the plains

That feel the chill breath of Niphæan hills,

He sang the loss of sweet Eurydice

And Pluto's bootless gift. And even when

The Thracian maidens maddened at the slight

Of their own beauty in such lasting grief

And wild from Bacchic orgies, slew the bard,

Strewing the broad fields with his severed limbs;

Then, even then, when Hebrus bore away

The tuneful head torn from the marble neck,

The cold lips, faithful still to their lost love,

Murmured, "Eurydice! Eurydice!"

And the sad banks replied "Eurydice!"

ADRIAN'S ADDRESS TO HIS SOUL.

(From Catullus.)

Animula! vagula, blandula,
Hospes, comesque corporis,
Quæ nunc abibis in loca,
Pallidula rigida, nudula
Nec, ut soles, dabis jocos?

The same rendered into English :

VERSION I.

Darling, gentle, wandering soul,
Long this body's friend and guest,
Tell what region is thy goal,
Pale and cold and all undrest,
Lost thy wonted play and jest?

N

VERSION II.

Spirit! sweet, gentle thing,
Thou seemest taking wing
For some new place of rest ;
So long this body's guest
And friend, dost thou forsake it,
And pallid, cold, and naked,
    Thou wanderest,
    Bereft of joy and jest,
Whither, ethereal thing?

VERSION III.

Dear, pretty, fluttering, vital thing,
    So long this body's guest and friend,
    Ah ! tell me, whither dost thou wend
        Thy lonely way,
Pallid and nude and shivering,
    Nor, as thy wont is, gently gay?

PYRAMUS AND THISBE.

(From Ovid's " Metamorphoses.")

Fairest of many youths was Pyramus,
And Thisbe beauteous among Eastern maids.
These dwelt in neighbour houses, where, of old,
Semiramis girt Babylon with walls.
And, being neighbours, these two fell in love,
And love with time grew stronger. They had wed,
But that their parents willed it not, and so
Forbade all intercourse. With mutual breasts,
Each sighed for other. Parted thus, they spoke ٬
By signs, and, being hindered, loved the more.

There was an opening in the common wall
That made their houses two, long unobserved,
But (what does not love see?) by them discerned.
Of this they made a passage for the voice,
And, safe from notice, murmured loving words.

As oftentimes they stood, the wall between,
Whispering and catching soft replies in turn,
"O envious wall, that standest in our way,.
Who love each other!" they would, vexed, exclaim,
"If thou would'st let us meet full face to face,
Or e'en enough to touch each other's lips!
And yet we are not thankless; 'tis to thee
We owe this pleasure of exchanging words."

Thus oft conversing, at approach of night,
They said "farewell," and kissed with longing lips,
That never met, the wall that stood between;
And when Aurora quenched the fires of night,
And Phœbus dried the dew upon the grass,
They came again unto the trysting place.

Once, having come and many plaints exchanged
Of their sad lot, they each with each agreed
To leave their homes, and in the silent night
Baffling their guardians, through the quiet streets,
Pass to the fields, and meet at Ninus' tomb.
There stood a tree with snow-white fruit adorned—
A lofty mulberry—a cool fount close by;

This was to be their trysting-place.

That day
Was slow to vanish in the western sea.
Then in the darkness Thisbe issued forth,
With stealthy footsteps, and with close-veiled face.
She reached the tomb, and 'neath the trysting-tree
Sat down (love made her confident); when, lo!
A lioness, her mouth all froth and blood,
From recent slaughter, came to quench her thirst
At the near fountain.

Thisbe saw her come,
(For the moon shone) and fled with frightened feet
Into a cave, and, running, dropt her veil;
Which, having quenched her thirst, the lioness,
Returning, found, and tore with bloody mouth.

Just then, came Pyramus with later feet,
Who saw the lion's tracks deep in the soil,
And paled with sudden fear. But when he found
His Thisbe's garment stained with blood, he cried,
"One fatal night two lovers shall destroy,

Of whom she was the worthier of life!
My soul is guilty, O dear perished love,
Who bade thee come at night to scenes of dread,
And let thee come the first. O lions! rush
From where you have your dens beneath the rock,
And tear these cursed limbs with ruthless teeth!
But — 'tis a coward's part to wish for death."

Then with the veil he seeks the trysting-tree,
And to its cherished folds gives kisses, tears,
And to his sword, "Drink now my blood," he cries,
And sinks it in his heart, and draws it forth,
And falling, lies at length with upturned face.
The blood spurts forth, as when a pipe that's burst
Throws from the hissing gap a slender jet,
Beating the obstant air with watery blows.
The trysting-tree is sprinkled with his blood,
Till its fair fruit is changed to gloomy black.

Then Thisbe, half afraid e'en yet, returns,
Lest Pyramus should miss her. Eagerly,
With eyes and heart, she looks for her beloved,
Burning to tell him of the danger past.

But when she gained the place and saw the tree
Sadly discoloured, she was sore in doubt
Whether or no it was the very spot;
Till, all aghast, she saw the blood-stained ground
And quivering limbs, and started, horror-struck,
Trembling as does the sea beneath a breeze.
And when she recognized her dear one's face,
She threw her tender arms above her head,
And tore her hair, and the dear form embraced,
Filling the wound with tears, and with her lips
Touched the cold face, and called him by his name;
" Pyramus, answer, thine own Thisbe calls!
Oh! hear me, Pyramus, look up once more!"
Touched by the voice, he oped his dying eyes,
Then closed them on the world for evermore.

She now saw all—her veil—the empty sheath.
" Ah! hapless love," she said, "hath slain my love,
But love will make me strong like him to die,
Fearing no wounds; for I will follow him,
The wretched cause—his comrade, too, in death:
And death that parted us shall re-unite.
O wretched parents of a wretched pair,

Whom true love bound together to the last,
Hear this, my dying voice, and not refuse
To let our ashes mingle in one urn.
O trysting-tree, whose funeral branches shade
The corse of one, and soon shall wave o'er two,
Henceforth forever be our mark of fate,—
Bear in thy fruit the memory of our death!"
She spake these words, and fell upon the sword,
And the point entered deep within her breast.
His blood, yet warm, was mingled with her own.

Her dying prayer the gods in heaven heard,
Her dying prayer touched the lone parents' hearts,
And both their ashes mingle in one urn.

THE WITHERED LEAF.

(From the French of A. V. Arnault.)

"De ta tige détachée."

"From thy branchlet torn away,
Whither, whither dost thou stray,
Poor dry leaf?"—"I cannot say.
Late, the tempest struck the oak,
Which was hitherto my stay.
Ever since that fatal stroke,
To the faithless winds a prey,
Not a moment's rest I gain.
From the forest to the plain,
I am carried by the gale.
Yet I only go the way
That the rose-leaf shuns in vain,
And where laurel-leaves grow pale."

ANDRÉ CHÉNIER'S DEATH-SONG.

André Chénier, for having dared to write against the excesses
of his countrymen, was summoned before the Revolutional Tri-
bunal, condemned and executed, in the year 1794. The first
eight stanzas (in the translation) he composed in prison, after his
condemnation ; the two last he wrote at the foot of the scaffold,
while waiting to be dragged to execution. He had just finished
the line, "Le sommeil du tombeau pressera ma paupière,"
when his turn came, and his words had their fulfillment. In the
translation, the spirit, not the letter, has been regarded.

When one lone lamb is bleating in the shambles,
    And gleams the ruthless knife,
His yester playmates pause not in their gambols,
    Their wild, free joy of life,

To think of him ; the little ones that played
    With him in sunny hours,
In bright green fields, and his fair form arrayed
    With ribbons gay and flowers,

Mark not his absence from the fleecy throng;
  Unwept he sheds his blood ;
And this sad destiny is mine. Ere long
  From this grim solitude

I pass to death. But let me bear my fate,
  And calmly be forgot ;
A thousand others in the self-same state
  Await the self-same lot.

And what were friends to me? Oh! one kind voice
  Heard through those prison-bars,
Did it not make my drooping heart rejoice,
  Though from my murderers

'Twas bought, perhaps? Alas! how soon life ends!
  And yet why should my death
Make any one unhappy? Live, my friends,
  Nor think my fleeting breath

Calls you to come. Mayhap, in days gone by,
  I, too, from sight of sorrow
Turned, careless, with self-wrapt unpitying eye,
  Not dreaming of the morrow.

And now misfortune presses on my heart,
    Erewhile so strong and free,
'Twere craven to ask you to bear its smart—
    Farewell, nor think of me!

*   *   *   *   *   *

As a faint ray or zephyr's latest breath
    Revives the dying day,
Beneath the scaffold, that stern throne of death,
    I sing my parting lay.

Before an hour, with wakeful foot and loud,
    Has marked its journey's close
On yon bright disc, the sleep of death shall shroud
    Mine eyes from worldly woes!

THE LAKE.

(From Lamartine.)

I.

For ever drifting towards shores unknown,
   In endless night, returnless, borne away,
We never, in Time's sea our anchor thrown,
   Pause for a single day!

II.

O Lake, I come alone to sit by thee,
   Upon the stone where thou didst see her rest,
Hardly a year ago, it seems, when she
   Looked on thy wavy breast!

III.

Thus didst thou threaten to those stooping rocks,
   Thus on their wave-worn sides thou then didst beat,
Thus did thy foam, aroused by windy shocks,
   Play round my darling's feet!

IV.

One evening, as we floated on the calm,
　And not a sound was heard afar or near,
Save oary music mingling firm and clear,
　With thy soft rippling psalm,—

V.

Then, all at once, sweet tones, too sweet for earth,
　Awoke the sleeping echoes into bliss,
The waves grew hushed, the voice I loved gave birth
　To such a strain as this:

1.

"O Time, suspend thy flight, and happy hours,
　　Linger upon your ways!
Oh! let us know the fleeting joy that's ours
　　These brightest of our days!

2.

For the unhappy ones who thee implore,
　　Flow swiftly as thou canst,
With all their cares; but leave us, pass us o'er
　　In happiness entranced!

3.

Alas! in vain I ask some moments more,
For Time escapes and flies!
I ask this night to linger; lo, the power
Of darkness quickly dies!

4.

But let us love, and, while we may, be blest,
Before our hour is gone!
Nor time, nor man has any point of rest,
It flows, and *we* float on!"

VI.

O jealous Time! those moments of delight,
When Love pours bliss in streams upon the heart,
Must they fly from us with as swift a flight
As days of ill depart?

VII.

Alas! can we not even mark the track?
Forever lost! like all that went before!
And Time that gave them and then took them back
Shall give them back no more!

VIII.

O Lake, mute rocks and caves and forest shade,
  Whose beauty Time is powerless to blight,
Dear nature, suffer not the thought to fade
  Of that sweet, happy night!

IX.

Still let it live in all thy scene, fair Lake,
  In calm and storm, and make thy smiles more bright,
And every tree and rock new meaning take
  From that sweet, happy night.

X.

Let it be heard in every passing breeze,
  And in the sound of shore to shore replying,
Let it be seen in every star that sees
  Its image in thee lying!

XI.

And let the moaning wind and sighing reed,
  And the light perfume of the balmy air,
All that is heard or seen or felt declare,
  " They loved—they loved, indeed!"

THE WANDERING JEW.

(From Beranger.)

I

Christian, a pilgrim craves from you
  A glass of water at your door !
I am—I am—the Wandering Jew—
  Chained to a whirlwind evermore !
Though ever young, weighed down with years,
  The end of Time my one glad dream ;
Each night I hope the end appears,
  Each morning brings its cursed gleam.
          Never, never,
Till this earth its race has run,
Shall my goal of death be won.

II.

For eighteen centuries, alas !
  Over the dust of Greece and Rome,

I've seen a thousand kingdoms pass,—
　And yet the end delays to come.
I've seen the good spring up in vain,
　I've seen the ill wax strong and bold,
And from the bosom of the main
　I've seen twin worlds succeed the old.
　　　　　Never, never,
Till this earth its race has run,
Shall my goal of death be won.

III.

God gives me life to punish me ;
　I cling to all that hopes for death,
But ere my soul's desire I see,
　I feel the whirlwind's vengeful breath.
How many a poor, sad man of grief
　Has asked from me the means to live !
But none from me has gained relief,—
　My hand has never time to give !
　　　　　Never, never,
Till this earth its race has run,
Shall my goal of death be won.

IV.

Alone, in shade of flow'ring trees,
    Upon the turf, where water flows,
If I enjoy a moment's ease,
    The whirlwind breaks my short repose.
Oh ! might not angry heaven allow
    One moment stolen from the sun !
Is less than endlessness enow ?
    Or shall this journey ne'er be done ?
           Never, never,
Till this earth its race has run,
Shall my goal of death be won.

V.

If e'er I see a child's sweet face,
    And in its pretty, joyous pride,
My own lost innocents' retrace,
    The Hoarse Voice grumbles at my side.
Oh ! you, who lust for length of days,
    Dare not to envy my career !
That sweet child-face on which I gaze
    Shall long be dust while I am here !

                              Never, never,
Till this earth its race has run,
Shall my goal of death be won.

VI.

I find some trace of those old walls,
    Where I was born long, long ago ;
I fain would stay, the whirlwind calls—
    " Pass on ! thy fathers sleep below,
But in their tombs no place is kept
    For thee ; thou still must wander on,
Nor sleep till all thy race has slept,
    And all the pride of man is gone."
                              Never, never,
Till this earth its race has run,
Shall my goal of death be won.

VII.

I outraged with a laugh of scorn
    The God-man in His hour of woe—
But from my feet the way is torn—
    I feel the whirlwind—I must go.

You, who feel not another's pain,
  Tremble—and help him while you can;
The crime I dared was foul disdain
  Not of God only, but of Man.
      Never, never,
Till this earth its race has run,
Shall my goal of death be won.

FINIS.

www.ingramcontent.com/pod-product-compliance
Lightning Source LLC
Chambersburg PA
CBHW020855270326
41928CB00006B/711